# Double Darrell

## Martin Bull

This book is dedicated to all the number 12's, Gasheads and Pirates, especially those who endured the many dark days of previous seasons.

**Double Darrell**

Published in the Independent Peoples' Republic of Wiltshire by shellshock publishing

Copyright 2016 © Martin Bull

First Edition - ISBN 978-0-9554712-9-2

# Introduction

Welcome to the pulsating story of Bristol Rovers' 2015-16 departure from League Two, as chronicled through the weekly-ish meanderings I had published on the Bristol Post web site. What an astonishing season, a veritable roller coaster of a ride, and for the third year in a row the last game of the season became a decider; a nail biting afternoon of squirm.

If you've not read any of my articles before, what can you expect from this book?

On a physical level you will encounter 45 juicy articles which are ENTIRELY unedited from what was written at the time (no hindsight for me; I will take my bad calls on the chin and accept any accolades to my heart), details of each match, QI stats, three special features, and eight pages of colour photos (mainly contributed by my fellow fans) plus a dozen or so colour photos in the 'football by footpath' adventures. Finally, unlike most evening reading, this book can positively guarantee a happy finish.

On a higher plain you will find Billy 'The Judge' Clark, Luddite history, Einstein, Neil Young, a mid 18th Century six seater privy, Prince, The Black Pearl, Ian Ogilvy, Jerel Ifil, Jordanian puns, Pulp, Harold Jarman, Albert Camus, De La Soul, Yeovil the Quisling of the West Country, Bowie, 'The Late Late Show', Paul 'Release the Beast' Nixon, R.E.M., President Harry S Truman (the 'S' stood for nothing at all; absolutely zilch), Barnstoneworth United, Shepshed Dynamo, Martin O'Neill's infamous conversation with Ray Kendall, Hereford FC's charming and inspiring motto, Mickey 'Plymouth Argyle Legend' Evans, the Chocolate derby, J.M.Coetzee, The Hollies, and last but not least, the legend that was Nathan Blissett.

I am an experienced terrace supporter who loves to write, likes to analyse, studied history and endeavours to dish up what my brother deliciously described as his 'five a day of culture'.

I hope YOU enjoy the result.

Please send any feedback to me at -
   hello@awaythegas.org.uk

**Martin Bull**

this book is number 184 of a signed limited edition of only 274 copies

# contents

# contents

# the answer my friend is blowin in the wind

## published on Friday 29th May 2015

⊗ **In recent Rovers news** ⊗

The six-day court case between Shamesbury's and BRFC concluded at the Royal Courts of Justice on 22nd May. Looking back it is quite amazing to recollect that the case started just two days before the Conference Play-Off Final at Wembley. If that fixture was called the most important match in our history, then the double whammy of a crucial court case at the same time shows just how much those involved at the club must have had on their plate.

Monday's open top bus tour of north and east Bristol to celebrate Rover's return to the Football League at the first time of asking was a handsome spectacle, with hordes of Gasheads lining the streets from Warmley to Lawrence Hill, followed by a sprint to Horfield to end up at the Memorial Stadium.

There were several personal highlights for me including watching the bus get stuck whilst trying to get through the narrow road into the Mem, at which point the trapped players engaged in banter with us Gasheads and started off their own rendition of the fan's song, "Everywhere we go, we're making all the noise". And five minutes later, whilst keeping ahead of the bus, I quite literally bumped into the Mayor and had an amiable chat before the bus disappeared into the forbidden zone. As a non-Bristolian the only reason I even recognised George Ferguson up-close was through a logical deduction that anyone wearing bright blue trousers must be the kind of person who is trying, slightly too hard, to cover up his usual daily attire of bright red ones.

Later, whilst taking photos on the pitch, I almost did a double take when being visually assaulted by someone scarily wrapped head to toe in ballooning white plastic sheeting and with 'Full of Gas' written in large letters on his chest - imagine if you can the Michelin Man and the Pillsbury Doughboy having an eccentric love child and you are somewhere in the vicinity of the spectacle.

These quirky moments demonstrated what a great event it was, full of families, flags, and ice creams melting down sticky toddler hands, and certainly a fittingly upbeat finale to what seemed like an exceedingly long and fraught season; as if most seasons following Rovers aren't.

It was therefore a complete surprise to later hear that the Daily Mirror had taken their eye off their own phone hacking problems and taken the trouble to pretend that a photo showing the players racing along an empty street on the way to the starting point of the tour at the old Warmley train station was showing maybe the "worst open top bus parade in history".

The Metro followed suit with the inflammatory tweet that "Bristol Rovers had an open-top bus parade but their fans couldn't really be bothered" and most disappointingly the web site of 'The Independent' followed along like a timid sheep, regurgitating the tired clichés that may be expected of a rotten red top, but not a quality broadsheet, adding the jab in the ribs that "Bristol Rovers had an average attendance of around 7,000 this season. ALI [sic] the glory hunters were at Wembley."

Fractious Gasheads quickly pointed out that aerial photos from the build-up to Chelsea's parade in West London were near identical to ours, yet the Mirror decided to applaud a photo of Chelsea youth players boarding their empty bus, and even interrupted their sycophantic live blog of that parade to take the mickey out of our celebrations, via THAT photo of our bus.

*We now interrupt that live blog to bring you an old folk tale from a rural Somerset village.*

Once upon a time a farmer fell out with his best friend and began spreading ugly rumours about him. Later, when he became ill and needed help to keep his farm running, he called upon the ex-friend and begged him for help with the daily milking. He came gladly, and was asked to forgive his ex-friend's slander. "I will happily help you and forgive you" the farmer said, "but there's something you must do. As soon as you get well, pluck the feathers from one of your chickens and scatter them in the marketplace and from the tower of the church; scatter them well throughout the entire village."

Later that month the farmer did just so, but still puzzled asked his neighbour if there was anything else he should do to repay his generosity. "Yes", he said, "Go and collect up all the feathers, making sure not one is missing." "But that is not possible!" the farmer cried, "the wind has carried so many of them away". "So it is with your words," his helper responded, "while I have forgiven you, please do not forget that you can never undo the damage your untrue words have done."

The Mirror article garnered almost 9,000 shares from their web site, and the Twitter stories from the three miscreants received 317 retweets, with 143 people also favouriting them. After pressure from Gasheads all three changed their stories, and apologised to varying degrees. The amended stories received 18 retweets, and 11 favourites.

Whilst this may not exactly be the most important issue on earth it is an interesting exploration into the mind set of some journalists, quick to get their facts wrong, to repeat stories without checking the evidence, and most significantly, to look down upon lower league and grass-roots football. And whilst these London-centric journalists pander to the lowest common denominator and follow with indecent haste the mantra that bigger is always best, they forget that small truly is beautiful.

Are they just following the arrogance of some fans of higher league football, or are they helping create and drive that arrogance?

It is hard to tell, and of course condescension is not confined only to supporters of Arsenal, Man United and the ilk, but permeates its way through all levels of football from the very top to the very bottom: Nottingham Forest fans looking down on Notts County fans; supporters of Football League teams looking down on non-league; or, a richer club looking down on a local rival.

If we learnt anything last season it was humility, coupled with the fact that the top level of non-league football is not wildly different from League Two; the main difference being the consistency of teams. These 'boundaries' are artificial, just as the differences between supporters of say, Bristol City, Bristol Rovers, and Bath City are rather synthetic, despite two divisions separating each team. We are actually quite similar, and we will all celebrate our own clubs achievements just as vociferously as Premier League fans will theirs.

# unsung heroes of promotion 2015 - part 1

## published mid June 2015

> ### ⊗  In recent Rovers news  ⊗
>
> ☠ The Beard (Stuart Sinclair) signs a new contract, possibly in real blood.
> ☠ Former Woking defender James Clarke joins on a one-year deal.
> ☠ Daniel Leadbitter signs a contract extension.
> ☠ Andy Monkhouse and Abdulai Bell-Baggie leave, soon to turn up at Grimsby Town and Stockport County respectively.

Over the next few weeks, amidst a dearth of transfer news and a player exodus to sunny climes unrivalled since the Israelites several millennia ago, I'll have a look at some of the (relatively) unsung heroes of our promotion season.

To hear that **Lee Brown**, our longest serving senior player (yes, and only 24 years old!) is contracted again to stay for our return to League Two got me scrabbling for the paragraphs I wrote about him this time last year, when I offered the opinion that Browner staying with the Pirates was the first fragment of genuinely excellent player news we had had since relegation. When I think of the attributes I want in a player he ticks all the boxes, including my slightly eccentric one about players not posting fatuous drivel on twitter or Facebook.  Lee has recently signed up to twitter, but his front page photo still may as well be a picture of tumbleweed rolling across a deserted Mid-West road, and long may that continue.

Mr. Brown seems to be an increasingly rare example of a young, modern day footballer who shuns the limelight and silly haircuts and just gets on with the job.  No whinging, no bad discipline and silly fouls, and no salacious rumours about his personal life.  Fit, healthy, never injured, properly left footed, honest, and loyal; what more can a fan want?  Lee also has an eye for a goal, can execute excellent free kicks and corners, and can even take penalties, admittedly with varying success on that front.  Given that he had missed his two previous pens, stepping up to be one the first five takers at Wembley just about summed up the man's rock-solid character.

Lee already has almost 200 appearances as a Pirate and has missed only a handful of games since being brought to us by the much maligned Paul Buckle. His exceptional three year partnership with Michael Smith suggests Buckle had more of a talent for spotting defenders than he did the splendid attributes of Bristolian's.

His first season saw him play 48 games, contribute seven goals and receive only three yellow cards. His next two seasons contributed 90 games, five goals and only five yellows, and after loyally staying with us following relegation he managed 47 games last season, two goals, not a card in sight and a squad leading nine assists. His seven assists for the 2013/14 season were also the highest in the squad, far more than Michael Smith's trio from the other side, just like his nine this season unquestionably outshone Tom Lockyer and Daniel Leadbitter combined on the right hand flank, with only a brace between them.

Most of us loyal Gasheads, myself included, will never really know how much credit the back-room staff deserve for last season, but it wouldn't be a wild stab in the dark to proffer some unsung accolades in the direction of **Steve Yates and Marcus Stewart**.

Although Scooter returned to his first love in 2013 as a 'mere' kit-man, it always seemed like a strangely under-whelming job proposal to be able to tempt an ex-Premier League player back from living abroad, and that maybe something else was bubbling under the surface of his Rovers return. It was therefore no surprise when he was later given the extra title of 'Defensive Coach' and although we may not know how much influence he had on this promotion team, 39 goals conceded in 52 games is unlikely to be a mere co-incidence.

As a muck about tough tackling centre back myself, forced to develop vision and positional sense to make up for less pace and height than Wee Jimmy Krankie, Steve Yates would be my role model as a centre back, the swift footed foil to the craggy solidity of Geoff Twentyman. But given that Yatesy never scored a goal for Rovers in 238 sublime appearances, it suggests that someone else may need to take some credit for Rovers' ever improving attacking ability last season.

If Steve Yates was the most talented defender I've ever seen in 26 years of supporting the Gas, Marco van Stewart was indisputably the most talented attacker. I will never forget his 1991 debut in a Rovers shirt, seven stone dripping wet, 3-0 down in the second half and up against the Nephilim defenders of Ipswich Town, the team who by the end of that season had won what is now called the Championship.

Instead of complaining about the rough-house tactics and playing into their hands, Stewie gave a performance akin to a shooting guard in basketball, going underneath the towering, lumbering centre backs and bagging his first ever League goal. A swift pair from 'Bruno' and Rovers, in Martin Dobson's first game as manager, had bravely fought back to 3-3. A star was born that very day, and his divinity was cemented just six days later when he scored a brace at Prenton Park, grasping the ball in the absence of Vaughan Jones to take a last minute pressure penalty to gain another important point.

Whilst Marcus has never been much of a scholar or a talker, Darrell Clarke sent him out to face the press more than ever before, and it seems rather unlikely that Rovers' enhanced attacking prowess, and slicker passing play last season, didn't include a large dollop of Stewie's glory days within this recipe for success.

Indeed it was always a mystery to Gasheads how our relegation season produced such blunt, insipid football, when we had Darrell (an attacking midfielder with over 60 career goals) and Stewie behind the scenes. The only logical conclusion seemed to be that John Ward had forgot that he himself was a potent striker in his own era, bagging a century of goals in less than 300 games, and curtailed the attacking sensibilities that oozed behind the scenes, with well over 400 career goals shared between that trio.

The moral of the story seems to be to let people be good at what they are good at.

No rocket scientists were harmed in the making of this promotion season, but quite a few stars were certainly born.

# unsung heroes of promotion 2015 - part 2

## published on Thursday 25th June 2015

---

⊗ **In recent Rovers news** ⊗

☠ Jake Gosling signs a contract extension, but refuses free eyebrow wax.

☠ Academy players Ryan Broom, Tyler Lyttle, Jay Malpas and Kieran Preston sign professional contracts.

☠ Angelo Balanta turns down a new contract and moves to Carlisle United instead. He probably doesn't realise just how close it is to Scotland.

---

Over the next few weeks, amidst a dearth of transfer news, I'm having a look at some of the (relatively) unsung heroes of our promotion season. Although recognised idols like Tom Parkes, Matty Taylor and Lee Mansell won't be featured, others will get their deserved moment in the spotlight.

I was saddened, although not surprised, when **Andy Monkhouse** decide to leave us this week in order to have a closer family life up North. Andy didn't win all Rovers' fans over, but he was a relatively unsung hero in my eyes, and will be seriously hard to replace.

First let me take you back to the Aldershot match in March. A mini slump had seen us lose top spot to Barnet, barbed discontent flew around the Blackthorn Terrace and the man behind us was very vocal in his opinion that Andy Monkhouse was a terrible player. When Monky made a mazy little run and executed a fine right footed finish (especially for an exceptionally left footed player), a group of guys in front of us turned to light-heartedly chide the detractor.

They evidently all knew each other, and even better came later when the Leeds-born wide man was named Man of the Match, and we all turned around and sang, "He's Man of the Match, he's Man of the Match, Andy Monkhouse, he's Man of the Match!" at his critic. It was all taken as banter, but it's not the first time a Rovers player has been loudly labelled rubbish by a vocal minority on the Blackthorn.

FIND A
STAMP
FOR
HERE
MUSH

Double Darrell - the book to end all Rovers' books - available via www.awaythegas.org.uk

Despite starting 41 games out of the 52 played last season, and playing in the same style each game, some Pirates made it all the way to Wembley whilst still expected him to be a traditional winger, hugging the by-line, taking people on for pace and skill, and providing probing crosses. He's never really been that type of operator and he certainly wasn't going be starting at 34 years old!

At 6' 2" Andy was surprisingly tall for a wide man, and certainly not the stature of the nippy winger we usually utilised on the opposite side of the pitch. And this is where the crux of his sporadic unpopularity lay. Not only were some fans disappointed that we rarely possessed two out and out wingers in our squad, but were also naïve to think that Darrell Clarke (or many managers for that point) would play a brace of them at non-league level anyway, as any 'perfect' wingers will be playing at a higher level, and the inherent imperfections of the ones left behind would be heavily punished.

Monky was a wide midfielder, and more comfortable with short passes than dribbles or balls over the top to run onto. To expect him to be Nathan Arnold or Simeon Akinola was unfair. In many ways he was actually more adaptable than such traditional fast men, also capable of being used as a forward and consistently exceptional in the air, with over 75 strikes in just over 400 starts (and 100 cameos as sub), and most of them coming at League One level.

Monky finished his brief Rovers career as our third top scorer, bagging eight league goals and two F.A. Cup wallops from the Dorchester thrashing. Many of them were important goals; each of his first four league strikes were the first Rovers goal of the match, and Rovers never lost a game he scored in, gaining 17 points out of the 21 on offer.

There was an obvious nagging similarity to Dave Savage and Jeff Hughes in that virtually every goal kick headed towards him on the left, to use his height. Moaners moaned incessantly at this tactic, but without the blessing of pace, his height was our only chance of ball retention from goal kicks, and was visibly just as important to the TEAM as the pace of Adam Dawson or the trickery of Lyle Della-Verda.

Similarly the partnership with Lee Brown behind him, sadly interrupted when Dave Martin was on the pitch, was just as important as, say, the centre-back relationship as they try to complement each other's strengths and weakness-es. And although Andy only had three goal assists to his name, the nine that

Lee Brown has been credited with must surely owe something to their distinctive left side partnership? From the other side Jake Gosling and Adam Dawson contributed only four between them, yet often received less disapproval that Monky's cautious style did.

As if to echo the analysis of Lee Brown last week, Monky was another fit, committed, serious, and disciplined player, and I wish him all the best in the twilight of his noteworthy career.

In the last throws of the season news came out of left-field that took Gasheads by surprise. Physiotherapist and ex-goalie, **Phil Kite**, had decided to retire at the end of the season, whether that be as sad Play-Off losers, or Wembley winners. Fortunately for us all it was the latter, and what a great way it was to send a first-rate servant out in style, plus a cherry on the cake when old team-mate Tony Pulis agreed to bring a strong West Bromwich Albion side down to the Mem for a Testimonial match on 31st July.

A local lad, who incidentally shares a birthday with my twin brothers, Phil signed as an apprentice for Rovers in 1980 and made his debut in January 1981 during the worst season in Rovers' entire history. He may have let in three that day, at Preston North End's romantic Deepdale, but Rovers had already scored four in the first half to record only their third victory of the 32 games thus far, and progress to the F.A. Cup Fourth Round. 119 League and Cup games later and Phil was off to Southampton in 1984, before eventually returning as Physio in 1996, under ex-apprentice colleague, and fellow Kingswooder, Ian Holloway.

Whether or not a Physio can really influence a team and thus be an unsung hero is a moot point of course, but we seemed to have less injuries than usual last season, and a Physio's role is surely just as much about enhancing morale and team spirit as anything else. I know that if I had the choice between a Phil Kite or a Paul Buckle in my dressing room, I'd have a Kitey every day. We hope to spot him standing on the terraces as a Gashead soon, but not in front of me please Phil, you're just too tall.

# unsung heroes of promotion 2015 - part 3

## published on Friday 26th June 2015

⊗ **In recent Rovers news** ⊗

Pirates mourned the loss of ex-player Gordon Fearnley. One of the original 'super subs' and utility players, Fearnley was limited to just less than 100 League starts in seven years, managing 21 goals. His Rovers QI stat was probably being the neglected scorer in the famous 8-2 demolition of a young Brian Clough's Brighton side in 1973; everyone remembers Smash & Grab's seven goals between them, but forget Gordon got the other.

Over the next few days and weeks, amidst a dearth of transfer news, I'm having a look at some of the (relatively) unsung heroes of our promotion season. Although recognised idols like Tom Parkes, Matty Taylor and Lee Mansell won't be featured, others will get their deserved moment in the spotlight.

I will freely admit that, along with the majority of modern football admirers, I am not the biggest fan of defensive minded full backs, but credit still has to be given to **Tom Lockyer**, not just for his can-do attitude and performances whilst out of position at right back, but also for being a genuine utility player, the likes of which modern football rarely gets to appreciate these days, just like no-one in this third Millennium wears wellies for the right reasons, and white dog poo has become strangely extinct.

Remarkably there are still some Rovers fans who don't see what a prospect this quiet lad is and have assumed that like a long line of home-grown youngsters before him, he'll probably end up on the scrap heap and down to local non-league football before you can cough Charlie Reece or Ben Swallow. Well, to paraphrase the golfer Arnold Palmer, 'the more times I make 49 starts in a season, the luckier I get'.

It certainly seems inconceivable that a virtual ever-present is there by fortune. Tom is only 20 years old and has already made a century of professional appearances, only seven of which have been from the subs bench, including his debut at Fleetwood Town in January 2013, so he's clearly never going to make it as a professional footballer.

Was it Oscar Wilde who said that sarcasm was the lowest form of wit? Maybe, but it's effective, just like Tom is.

Personally I felt that playing a centre back at right back, a brace of relatively uncreative central midfielders, and a somewhat pedestrian left midfielder in the shape of Andy Monkhouse, gave us an overly cautious approach for too much of last season, but that is not to criticise Tom himself, or the role he has been asked to play in a squad that did not ooze conspicuous creativity.

Not blessed with the pace of Leadbitter, the physicality and growing ball skills of Parkes, or the big-man marking expertise that Macca possesses, Tom may still be finding his most effective position in football, but whilst he does he gives wholehearted and efficient performances wherever he is asked to perform, and has shown maturity far beyond his years. Even his questionable disciplinary record improved as the season went on, another sign of a boy becoming a man.

Whilst our back five last season may have been rock steady and able, containing most of the same personnel who were ranked as the 10th best defence in a relegation season, that could not always be said for our frontline or the troublesome right wing position. It is easy to forget that pre-season was hardly a perfect period, forcing Darrell Clarke to bring in numerous **loan signings** as early as mid August. Whilst I don't believe any of them alone warrants cult hero status, all played their part, and even the relatively unsuccessful ones were warmly welcomed into the club, gave us as good at they possessed at the time, and left with best wishes and sincere 'thank you' messages from Gasheads all over the world.

**Adam Cunnington** and **Dave Martin** were brought into the club as soon as the season started going downhill fast, and both had some genuinely excellent matches. Cunnington was possibly our best loan signing for many years, scoring three excellent goals and offering us a brand of striker the squad simply didn't possess until Nathan Blissett was snaffled up in mid-November.

Although Martin started well, he clearly couldn't hit a barn door with a banjo and left the team very left footed, with Monkhouse rather wasted by his relocation to the right. His final appearance, against Kidderminster Harriers, actually represented a mini-turning point in the thinking of Darrell Clarke.

Whilst **Lyle Della-Verde** was making his first start for Rovers, Martin and Jamie White were both unceremoniously hauled off at half-time, with Ryan Brunt following 16 minutes later.

None of them ever played in the league again for Rovers. It was certainly a ruthless case of out with the old and in with the new and we lost only one more league game after that. Della-Verde and **Adam Dawson** were both young players with pace and tricks. Not always the best decision makers and sometimes as frustrating as guiding a toddler along a busy pavement, they nonetheless terrorised defenders, got in crosses and gave us traditional wing-play that excited us loyal Gasheads.

It's all too easy to overlook the reality that watching Rovers last season was generally a pretty dull existence until snowdrops and crocuses appeared, and even then several games bored us to tears until Easter saw a real blossoming of our slick attacking prowess.

The lack of appreciation in some quarters for the so-called less creative Brown and Monkhouse partnership is summed up by the fact that Daniel Leadbitter, Jake Gosling, Lockyer, Martin, Della-Verde and Dawson scored only five goals between them, whereas the left side duo had 12 between them, with a dozen assists thrown in as well.

It almost seems unfair to compare these mainly young, unknown loanee's with **Chris 'one of our own' Lines**, a League One runner-up with Sheffield Wednesday, but as a loanee Chris does deserve a special mention in this section. Last season any Gashead could have detected that from day one we lacked a creative ball carrier in central midfield, so our tails were well and truly raised when it was announced that Chris would be returning for the final eight games of the season, and into the play-offs if needed.

In a league that went to the wire, Chris may well have been that vital, if expensive, cog that made the whole machine tick slickly towards promotion, and we certainly became far more creative with him in the side whilst still managing to be the third most frugal defence in the top five divisions of English football.

# unsung heroes of promotion 2015 - part 4

## published on Friday 3rd July 2015

⊗ **In recent Rovers news** ⊗

☠ Will Puddy agrees a contract extension.

☠ Neal Trotman rejects the opportunity to use pre-season at Rovers to build up his fitness following injury, so was officially released. A year later he tweeted that he is "retired due to injury", but it's not clear exactly when he sadly decided to call it a day.

In the last few weeks I've been having a look at some of the (relatively) unsung heroes of our promotion season.

In the absence of any completely unsung heroes playing up front I have created a little section for some of the best finishes of the promotion year.

I was disappointed for most of the season at how little game time **Ellis Harrison** was given, alongside some of the lazy old-fashioned stereotypes used against him, leading him to be pigeonholed as a 'super sub', an equally lazy concept. Darrell Clarke didn't make many mistakes last season, but to hand starts to players like Alex Wall, Bradley Goldberg, Jamie White and Ryan Brunt directly ahead of Harrison was one of them; 12 starts and 16 sub appearances between them, yet not one goal.

Scoring eight goals as a sub, four of which directly won the game for Rovers, sadly propelled Ellis into a bizarre Catch 22 netherworld where he was kept in a dungeon as a 'super sub' as if not to tempt some incomprehensible witches curse. Harrison possesses a rare mix of pace, strength, enough height, and, most important, deadly finishing. He is easily the best finisher in the squad and I would trust him with a 1-on-1 with the keeper like I used to trust Jamie Cureton in his pomp. To score 17 goals from only 10 starts and 29 entrances from the bench (the later at an average of only 23 minutes per appearance), was an amazing show-case for his talents, and given a smidgen less than 1,500 minutes on the grass all season, those 17 strikes work out at a goal every 87 minutes played. That puts his season up there, statistically, with 'The Black Pearl'; Eusébio, and Edson Arantes do Nascimento; Pelé.

Whilst Harrison's finishes against Lincoln City (away) and Chester (home) would be in the top drawer, his sublime control and volley to grab a last minute draw at FC Halifax Town, on a rotting badger of a pitch, was off the scale, and would have easily graced a World Cup match. It is still quite amazing to look back and find that Ollie Clarke, Chris Lines, Adam Cunnington and Dave Martin all made more starts than Ellis, and Jake Gosling, Nathan Blissett and Daniel Leadbitter all made at least twice as many starts.

Goals to make Gasheads skip a heartbeat were also dished out by **Jake Gosling**, with two sweet strikes into the top corner, against Southport and Alfreton Town. These not only showed beautiful balance and poise, but suggested that whilst the tired cliché of a left footed right winger cutting infield to curl in a pearler may be a predictable tactic, it is hard to stop when executed with such precision.

If Association Football allowed temporary specialists onto the pitch the way American Football does, we would have **Ollie Clarke** down on the roster as a long range shooting expert.

Although his single handed flattening of plucky AFC Telford United, both home and away, were his most important goals of a stop-start season, they were simply pedestrian compared to his blaster to level the scores against Gateshead, and my personal Goal of the Season, his clever 35 yarder at Eastleigh to catch the goalie away from his native soil and rescue a point when down to 10 men.

Of course certain followers of tiny red breasted birds will laugh at the idea of a game at Eastleigh being a great memory to evoke, but they will miss not only the fact that a quirky away day-out is the bread and butter of all true fans at all levels, but also that our season in the Conference was a penance we had to go through to begin to atone for our arrogance and mistakes in the past, just like 1982 will forever be etched in the conscience of those twitchers from BS3.

# unsung heroes of promotion 2015 - part 5

## published on Thursday 9th July 2015

> ⊗ **In recent Rovers news** ⊗
>
> ☠ Chris Lines agrees a permanent move to Rovers, thus bringing his career full circle, like a big round circley thing.
> ☠ Jamie Lucas and Danny Greenslade both agree contract extensions.
> ☠ Cristian Montaño signs for Rovers after time out in Colombia.

Today a final crop of rich pickings have their deserved moment in the spotlight.

Although **Neal Trotman** was not offered a new contract, he was given the chance to stay until his injury cleared, and as no bridges have been burnt by either side I'm sure there will be a warm welcome if we ever see him again in the famous blue and white quarters.

Given that most fresh memories of Mark McChrystal are of him steadily improving since New Year and then wearing the Captain's armband as he lifted the Play-Off Winners Trophy at Wembley, it is easy to forget that until Neal Trotman's injury at the New Bucks Head on the opening day of November Trotters was actually the preferred partner to seasonal ever-present Tom Parkes at the heart of the most frugal defence in the Conference, nay the most parsimonious Rovers defence since the 33 goals conceded by the famed 1973/74 promotion winning side. Darrell Clarke, yet again, has to take some of this credit as Macca had played all 270 minutes of the first three games of the season, but after the trip up to Altrincham, and only one point from three games, he took the fearless decision to drop his Captain and keep him on the bench until an opening arose.

As Trotman's 19 league appearances all came at the beginning of a season that didn't exactly get off to the best of starts, it is a testament to his old fashioned rugged Centre Back style that we gained an impressive 1.89 league points per game with him in the team, which is far closer to the full season league average of 1.98 points per game than many Gasheads may have expected.

☠

A sure-fire unsung hero of our promotion wore the **Number 12** shirt. A loud character, well respected in football circles, well travelled, passionate, and always available in any weather, but whinged occasionally, was often a spectator, and lacked confidence at times. The instant promotion meant a huge amount to him... and her, and the dog, because number 12 is allocated to the Gasheads themselves, and by God we deserved it for enduring those five previous seasons!

Although I was always confident Gasheads would not desert their team, even in non-league, it shouldn't be taken for granted that not only did overall attendances rise, but the amount of Gasheads in the Mem rose even higher because the number of away fans visiting Horfield was slashed in half. There was also an official average of 867 Gasheads travelling to each regular season or Cup away game, where we provided 34% of the total crowd despite a longer than usual 293 mile average round trip (from Bristol), lots of all-ticket restrictions, Tuesday night matches and other obstacles (see page 185). It's easy to forget that we rarely won games easily and only sporadically provided excitement for money until the end of the season.

The recent talk of a possible foreign-backed take over of the club actually made me more proud to be one of the Number 12's at the club. Long derided for being a backwater in English football, the reasons given why someone could be interested in investing in Bristol football put a glow in my cheeks.

Instead of all the usual pessimism and misery about how Rovers were under-achieving, badly run, and at an aging stadium not built with football in mind (admittedly all sadly true!), it was nice to feel wanted, despite that huge hairy wart slap bang on the middle of our hooter.

As much as I love the laid back, unassuming and self-effacing Bristolian style, we do occasionally need to get a box of pound shop party poppers out and comprehend just how attractive we could be.

A huge fan base in a massive City, with little English football competition for many miles around, and currently playing two levels below what could be sustainable with the right governance and the right stadium. That is essentially quite an attractive proposition, especially when considering so many other teams have to exist in smaller catchment areas.

Although I would love to go through a huge list of unsung volunteers, support-ers club stalwarts, and even paid staff who often go well beyond the call of duty (you know who you are!), it would be slightly off the remit of this series as I really did hope to concentrate solely on players, plus any backroom staff who are in a position to have a more direct impact on player performance on the pitch.

It is therefore maybe fitting to finish on the Mem's un spoilt pitch itself. Groundsman **Eric Kingscott** and his merry band of pixies and match day volunteers worked so hard to give us a literal bowling green of a pitch at the Mem. This suited our style of play and with the best home record in the league it certainly seemed to be yet another unsung hero for us.

The beauty of league football is that it is a true test of the resilience of a squad, their tactics and their leadership. 46 games spread over eight months, home and away, Bank Holidays and Christmas congestion, a Tuesday evening in Wrexham and a Friday night under the lights, in all weathers and on all pitches.

Knowing that 23 of these games would be on an even surface, full of grass, benefited us and our struggles on the appalling surfaces of FC Halifax Town and Dartford, and the rock hard slope at Dover, made us appreciate the Mem even more.

**So, here's a toast to the unsung heroes of a memorable promotion season. I hope we will find even more of them to venerate next season.**

# special feature
## an interview with www.the92.net

**www.the92.net - Bouncing back at the first attempt is no mean feat – obviously you're delighted – did you always feel you had enough to get the job done?**

Martin Bull - Just. With the sort of start Barnet had (including a 5-0 away win on the opening day!), and the sort of start we had (1 point from 9 available, and serious pressure on our manager), it never looked like we would have a chance of automatic promotion until glimmers of hope came in the New Year. I always had supreme faith in our manager, Darrell Clarke, and once we got into the play-off positions in October, we never looked like leaving them and as we became a TEAM, we really developed into the strongest side in them. Finishing second, with 91 points, only 5 losses, and no away loss since September, gave us real confidence when the play-offs finally arrived, and even a sense of entitlement. I feel that overall it was a fair result for us to scrape through at Wembley, even though we didn't play well. Most Gasheads would have loved the Mariners to have joined us, but only two promotion slots is a brutal system.

**Did you manage to get to many non-league grounds during your season in the Conference?**

Not many. I love away games and have recently edited and published a book about them, 'Away The Gas', but with two young kids to entertain I only managed Eastleigh, Aldershot Town, Woking, Dover Athletic and Forest Green Rovers. They were all cracking away days though and I didn't see a loss, which was a bonus considering that in the previous season our away record was the worst in League Two.

**What was your best and your worst memory from your non-league travels?**

All my five away days were really great little adventures, many of which I wrote about via my weekly article on the Bristol Post web site. FGR in the Play-offs was the best memory. It was the only win I saw and a dominant performance very successfully calmed the nerves. The penultimate league game at Dover Athletic's Crabble was a first-rate day out off the field but the result was a choker.

A dodgy last minute equaliser awarded to the Whites quite literally snatched automatic promotion out of our hands. To come back from that and win the Play-offs showed a lot of mental strength.

The best 'result' that came from our away travels in non-league though was the restoration of our reputation as mainly decent, loyal, funny, and passionate (sometimes annoying!) fans.

We made a lot of friends last season and a little humility went a long way, especially compared to other so-called 'big' clubs who had found themselves in a league they thought was beneath their history. We are a huge dock City with large areas of social deprivation, so we're not all cuddly teddy bears, but the mass majority of us were courteous and humble, loved our time in non-league, and didn't look down our noses at other clubs. We deserved to be there, just like all the other 23 teams.

It's a shame we couldn't have developed those relationships even more, but there is no way we could have passed up the opportunity of an immediate exit. Sorry non-league fans, we learnt so much, and we love your loyalty, but we just had to desert you.

**Do you think the club is in a better position now than say 18 months ago (6 months pre-relegation)?**

Good God yes! We slept walked to relegation, although in our defence we went down on goal difference and were only in the relegation zone for 54 minutes of the entire season. In the 2014/15 season those 50 points would have seen us safe by nine points.

Promoted clubs tend to have an excellent next season and I'm a firm believer in stable, successful teams being well placed to continue their upsurge. In Darrell Clarke we have the best young manager in the England. He genuinely has 'given us our Rovers back' and is my kind of guy. Principled, honest, frank, open to new ideas, financially prudent, brave, tough on discipline, with strong morals, and sometimes opinionated and prickly. The fact that he twice ended up drinking with Rovers fans towards the end of the season spoke volumes; he really is 'one of us' and immerses himself in his job. And yet he still doesn't always get the credit he deserves because his success has 'only' been in non-league. Three promotions in four years as a manager. Not bad for a 37 year old!

**There have been a number of rumours surrounding ground redevelopment/new stadia over the years – and some major developments in the last few weeks - what's the latest on this and where does that leave the club?**

A High Court case went against us last week, which has pretty much scuppered all our chances of a new stadium. Four years of successful planning applications, careful community relations, challenges, Courts, and expensive lawyers; all down the drain, based on one tiny line in a labyrinthine contract, and more importantly the fact that Sainsbury's didn't want to honour the contract they had signed, nor show any interest in sorting the impasse out.

Plan B is well... we don't have one. That innovative stadium idea, a collaboration with the rapidly expanding University of the West of England, was genuinely so perfect and astute that it looked like we finally entering the 21st Century... until delays, a Green Party funded NIMBY group, and the economy intervened. The annoying thing is that we probably only need about £15m extra to get a beautiful stadium built but it's just £15m extra we don't have without Sainsbury's buying our current ground, and our Board have already maxed out their funds. Meanwhile City have a billionaire 'local boy made good' owner who could tip a wine waiter £15m and not realise it was gone.

Oh well, we aren't called Rovers for nothing. We'll endure until the next plan comes along.

**How many of the current 92 grounds have you visited?**

Ah ha. Controversy. I think your rule that it has to be the current ground of the club in question is unfair. With 'only' 67 of the current 92 clubs visited since Reading vs. Bristol Rovers at Elm Park on 21st November 1989, and now with two young kids, no cash and many of the furthest Northern ones left, I know it'll probably take me another 10 years or so to finish this miniature aspiration, even on my rules. I've been to Gay Meadow, Millmoor, the Goldstone Ground, Layer Road and others, but not to Greenhous Meadow, the New York Stadium, the Amex and whatever that Colchester carbuncle is called. I don't see why I should be forced to re-visit those clubs as, in all good faith, I did watch a competitive game of football (nearly always a League game, and certainly never a friendly) at the ground that was their home at that point in time.

Using your rules I'm back down to 56. Let's just hope Carlisle United don't move ground!

**Which grounds will you be aiming to visit over the coming season?**

Given my current circumstances I'm probably looking at a handful of away trips this season. A few with my best friend who is a Norwich City fan (Leicester City and Stoke City maybe), and a few with Rovers, where I strangely have a couple of local grounds I've not yet been to; Yeovil Town, and Newport County's current tenure at the rugby stadium. Plus one further jaunt to try to visit a more Easterly one; Notts County or Mansfield Town maybe. Despite relegating us, the Stags have sort of become our friends.

I already have a 'football by footpath' route mapped out for our country bumpkin cousins at Yeovil Town. This blog is one of my little projects; the quirky way to arrive at an away match, usually involving a smidgen of research, a public footpath or a canal towpath, shanks' pony, a pub and preferably decent weather. Falling down hills and getting lost is also distinctly possible, but it's hardly an extreme sport, so hand glider geeks and parachutists need not apply.

**Finally – what can fans visiting the Memorial Stadium next season look forward to?**

Alas it's exactly the same as before! No improvements have been made to the 'The Mem' for around a decade as we've had two really excellent plans that fell at the final hurdle (first one re-development, second one the new stadium - both with planning permission agreed), meaning it has been illogical to spend money on what little we already have.

The pasties are still good, the terrace is still quite big (and open - sorry but you might be hearing us singing 'Getting wet, Getting wet' at you), the section of away seats are still quite an awful view, but at least it isn't an anonymous out-of-town off-the-shelf stadium that has no pubs, no easy parking, and no quirkiness. The Mem is nothing if not quirky - six different sections that were thrown up in the air by a giant and landed higgledy-piggledy back down to earth.

# the road is long, with many a winding turn

### published on Thursday 23rd July 2015

---

*Saturday 11th July - 1st Pre-season Friendly*

### Salisbury 1    Bristol Rovers 4

Coulson - 89'      Lucas - 12' & 57',
                    Blissett - 52' & 90'

**Rovers:** Mildenhall, Tyler Lyttle, Lockyer (Alfie Kilgour - 69'), McChrystal, Danny Greenslade, Cristian Montaño (Jay Malpas - 69'), Sinclair (Dominic Thomas - 59'), Gosling (Ryan Broom - 69'), Bodin, Blissett, Jamie Lucas.

Attendance: 1,068 inc 386 Gasheads.   Referee: Brendan Malone

---

*Sunday 12th July - 2nd Pre-season Friendly*

### Sutton United 1    Bristol Rovers 1

Collins - 83'      Lines - 15', Broom - 80'

**Rovers:** Kieran Preston, Leadbitter, J. Clarke (Alfie Kilgour - 66'), Parkes, Brown, Jennison Myrie-Williams, Lines (Dominic Thomas), O. Clarke, Toby Ajala, Harrison (Jay Malpas - 51'), Taylor (Ryan Broom - 46').

Attendance: 658.

---

*Tuesday 14th July - 3rd Pre-season Friendly*

### Cirencester Town 0    Bristol Rovers 7

Bodin - 7', 16' & 41',
Lucas - 33' (pen), 59', & 81'
(pen), Broom - 61'

**Rovers:** Mildenhall, Lyttle, Lockyer (Kilgour - 46'), McChrystal, Greenslade, Broom, Sinclair (Malpas - 60'), Mansell (Jake Slocombe - 60'), Gosling, Lucas, Bodin.

Attendance: 201.   Referee: Adam Matthews

*Wednesday 15th July - 4th Pre-season Friendly*

## Mangotsfield United  0    Bristol Rovers  2

Blissett - 31' & 60'

**Rovers:** Preston, Leadbitter, J. Clarke (Slocombe - 70'), Kilgour, Parkes, Brown, O. Clarke (Malpas - 70'), Lines, Toby Ajala, Harrison, Blissett.

Attendance: Estimated by Mangos as 1,500+   Referee: Mark Dadds

---

*Saturday 18th July - 5th Pre-season Friendly*

## Bristol Rovers  0    Arsenal Under-21's  1

Mavididi - 5'

**Rovers:** Mildenhall, Leadbitter, J. Clarke, Parkes, Greenslade (Malpas - 76'), Sinclair (Montaño - 60'), Lines, Mansell (O. Clark - 46'), Gosling, Harrison (Taylor - 46'), Bodin (Easter - 60').

*Unused Substitutes:* Blissett, Lucas.

Attendance: 2,093 inc 150 glory hunters.   Referee: Kevin Johnson

---

*Tuesday 21st July - 6th Pre-season Friendly*

## Bristol Rovers  0    Reading  2

Samuel - 39', Blackman - 65'

**Rovers:** Mildenhall, Leadbitter (Lyttle - 46'), J. Clarke (Kilgour - 75'), Parkes, Brown (Greenslade - 46'), Sinclair (Malpas - 63'), O. Clarke, Lines (Gosling - 46'), Montaño (Bodin - 56'), Taylor (Blissett - 63'), Easter (Harrison - 46')

*Unused Substitutes:* Preston, Lucas.

Attendance: 1,880 inc 264 Royals.   Referee: Kevin Johnson

---

Obviously we are all incredibly frustrated that Sainsbury's have won the first battle in the legal case over the contract to buy the Mem. I write the 'first battle' because the law is a complicated beast and an appeal is imminent.

I must admit that my initial reaction to the dreadful news was 'please don't appeal, it's just lawyers getting rich and making us look pathetic', but that very same day the top news story in Wiltshire was the complex and unseemly case of which Council will be forced to pay for a young man who lives with serious disabilities and will require costly personal care for the rest of his life.

The Department of Health initially said Cornwall Council [where his parents and siblings live] should pay, and that ruling was upheld by the High Court.

The Court of Appeal later reversed that decision, saying that South Gloucestershire [where he has lived with foster parents most of his life] should pick up the bill.

The Supreme Court has now ruled that Wiltshire Council [where he was born] has to pay his £80,000 a year care bill.

That case suggests that not only is the road long, with many a winding turn, but there is also no return at this point. So on we go because plan B is well... we don't have one. That innovative stadium idea, a collaboration with the rapidly expanding University of the West of England (UWE), was genuinely so perfect and astute that it looked like we were finally entering the 21st Century... until delays, TRASHorfield, and the economy intervened.

The frustrating thing is that we probably only need about £15m extra to get a beautiful stadium built, with many local benefits, but it's just £15m extra we don't have without that Sainsbury's contract, and our Board seem to have already maxed out their credit cards. Meanwhile City have a billionaire 'local boy made good' owner who could tip a wine waiter £15m and not realise it was gone.

Oh well, supporting Rovers is always more a twisty country road than an efficient autobahn. The clue is in our name, and compared to the struggles others have in life it's no burden to bear. We'll get there sometime, who knows when, but as the planning permission on the UWE Stadium doesn't run out until 17th January 2018 I wonder if there may even be some chance of a new funding plan coming out of the left-field, if the Uni can wait that long?

At the risk of being labelled an ostrich by a recently sacked football manager, I enjoyed our away day to the resurrected Salisbury F.C. last week, and the great turn-out from over 1,000 Whites fans and Gasheads. If any fans know what it is like to have a really tumultuous five years, it is a Whites loyalist, enduring a roller coaster of administration, an enforced double relegation, two promotions, and finally liquidation and an entire season without even a club. For us at least the football goes on and we'll try to enjoy what we do have rather than be too depressed about what we don't have (yet?).

As the Ray Mac Stadium is miles outside the centre of Salisbury, and was pretty much on its tod until new houses began to surround it, I assumed that this would be perfect territory for a 'football by footpath' saunter.

'football by footpath' is one of my little projects; the quirky way to arrive at an away match. The full 'Old Sarum Stroll' is re-printed over the next six pages, complete with some of the photos I used in the blog.

I already have a route mapped out for our opening away trip of the new season to our country bumpkin cousins at Yeovil Town. Now I just need to be able to secure a ticket. *[Note - I did get a ticket and the 'football by footpath' article for it is reprinted on pages 50 to 55].*

I was very impressed by the new thinking of splitting the squad into two separate friendlies, and giving most of them a proper match and a chance to gel, rather than the old 'first half with one team, second half with another' routine. Seven of our starting 11 played a full 90 mins in this first pre-season match, and some, like Nathan Blissett and Jamie Lucas, were still running like gazelle's at the end. We did struggle a bit when the three youngster subs came on, but obviously they were introduced precisely because we were well ahead and it was an apt time to give them a crack at a real match.

As usual it was great to be able to attend a free Q&A with Darrell Clarke even if it slightly suffered from that unique Bristol Rovers manner of organisation. 90 minutes of non-stop questions, answers and chat are almost impossible to cover on paper, but what is actually more noteworthy is that the session proved yet again what many of us have known all along; what a meticulous, passionate, modern, strong, honest, clever, and tough taskmaster Darrell is. We are very fortunate to have him. Gone are the days of a 55 year old bloke with little recent knowledge of English football commuting from Brighton, or a jumped up Napoleon figure trying to push his players and staff around.

We finally have a leader, an intelligent modernist, and a man manager; a Renaissance man born on a dodgy Council estate in Mansfield.

## special feature

# football by footpath

### *Salisbury F.C. vs. Bristol Rovers F.C.*

Pre-season Friendly - 11th July 2015

Raymond McEnhill Stadium, Partridge Way, Old Sarum, Wiltshire, SP4 6PU

What better way to celebrate the new Salisbury F.C.'s first ever pre-season friendly at the 'Ray Mac' Stadium, than to (a) play Bristol Rovers, and (b) go for a wander?

It may not seem obvious to the casual observer but Bristol Rovers 'owe' a huge debt of gratitude to Salisbury F.C., or technically its direct predecessor, the liquidated Salisbury City F.C.. Their most successful manager, Darrell Clarke, jumped ship to Rovers in June 2013, possibly spotting that the problems that had seen them demoted two divisions in the summer of 2010 where still not entirely over, even though DC had been the man, with Mikey Harris, to get them back to the Football Conference's highest level with two gritty play-off promotions in three heady seasons. If Salisbury were back to the 5th Tier of football, and playing in front of 1,000 fans in a decent new stadium, why leave for a basket case club trading on its former glory?

To Gasheads it was always a curious move. Hot young manager at the most successful local-ish non-league club, taking a demotion to be an assistant only one division higher? Immediately from his appointment, which apparently started from a chance phone call and was not part of any plan as such (the words 'plan' and 'Bristol Rovers' rarely do go together), most Rovers fans assumed he was being groomed as a Head Coach in the near future, whilst old dinosaur John Ward would move upstairs to be a comfy, well paid, Director of Football.

That concept just about sums Rovers up. Although John Ward had done well in 2013 to rescue Rovers from yet another terrible first half to a season, there seemed to be no real logic for him staying to be a hands-on 'Manager' when various evidence seemed to suggest a younger man was needed. Anyway, the assumption is that DC came to Rovers either on the tacit understanding he could well end up as Head Coach or Manager very soon, or on the general feeling that Rovers will be the better long term prospect for an ambitious and successful young manager, who was popular and loyal where ever he had been employed in his career thus far.

It was of course a marriage made in Hades and Rovers were relegated to non-league football for the first time since they joined the Football League in 1920. I'll spare you the details as this is supposed to be about walking to football grounds, not walking into an abyss with your eyes wide closed; the point being that part of the deal to let DC join Rovers included a minor money spinning pre-season friendly for Salisbury.

This friendly, which brought 1,068 fans through the doors, including at least 386 Pirates, was therefore a conclusive 'thank you' to the Whites, and a fitting homecoming for a man who graced the club as a player/manager for six years. Rovers had also plundered his ex-team when they sadly went out of business in July 2014 and although Jamie White proved to be a flop at the Gas and had already moved on to lower things, and Will Puddy was injured and unable play, cult hero Stuart 'The Beard' Sinclair did start the game, making his comeback from injury at his old club. How perfect.

As The Beard is omnipotent it was no surprise that he survived 60 mins untouched by human hands and was only subbed to give his luxuriant whiskers a well deserved rub down and ice bath. I almost wished I had smuggled my 'Beard' sign (recently liberated from a certain builder and pictured below) into the stadium to greet his return to action.

DC is clearly the best thing to happen to Bristol Rovers for many, many years, not just because of the results, but more importantly because of the ethos he brings, and the modern thinking that permeates his approach to all aspects of running a football operation; a Renaissance man born on a dodgy Council estate in Mansfield. I would therefore walk over broken glass and have my hair almost shaved off by a small plane for this man of men, and I quite literally did.

As the Ray Mac is miles outside the centre of Salisbury, and was pretty much on its tod until new houses began to surround it, I assumed that this would be perfect territory for a 'football by footpath' saunter. I had been to Old Sarum before, the ancient pre-Salisbury settlement just a flints throw away, so to be able to link all three together in an afternoon was like a dream come true. If Tony Robinson wasn't a dirty red I might have even roped him along for the ride into bygone times.

A quick look on a map offered me a starting point at the hamlet of Ford, set off of a Roman road that leads from the Iron Age hill fort they used to occupy. Any fellow football footpather can follow my footsteps by parking on any of the roads in Ford, such as Merrifield Road or Manor Farm Road, circa SP4 6DX.

Then walk due North up the official footpath (Green Lane), past Manor Farm, or even better use the now closed road that takes you parallel to the lane, but right on the edge of Old Sarum airfield itself, which slightly surprisingly shows evidence that Salisbury has at least one spotty scroat who has ambitions to be a graffiti writer when he gets better at his craft.

Old Sarum airfield is one of only three in England that has been in continuous use as a grass flying field since its construction during World War I, and is the only one of the three currently in civilian use and open to the public. It also has three of the four original World War I hangars still standing, all of which are Grade II* listed buildings.

The perimeter road you'll be walking on passes right next to the Eastern end of the airstrip, with only a hedge of young trees separating you from the runway, so if you are fortunate enough to time your trip perfectly you'll get the thrill of planes flashing 15 metres above your noggin whilst seconds from landing. They are so close you can see what religion the pilot is. Maybe...

My walk to the football fortunately coincided with a pilot doing take-off and landing practice so I witnessed him go up and round and down several times. On the way back later a throng of parachutists looked incandescent as they slowly circled down to earth out of the moody, sun drenched clouds (pictured below).

Once you've left the airfield behind you'll be into the edge of Old Sarum Business Park, coming out onto the main road (the Portway) sandwiched between the Land Rover / Range Rover dealership and a Skoda / Kia counterpart. There is a short cut to the football ground by crossing straight over the road, into Sherbourne Drive, where the new Charles Church housing estate is. You know it must be Charles Church because each house has their name written into the front of the house near the door, as if a 'Charles Church' plaque was a modern day equivalent of 'Dunroamin', 'Wynding Down' or 'Llamedos' (think about it... or just use reverse gear). As an avowed hater of advertisers shoving their pathetic ads right in our faces in public places, I'd be quite happy if a local juice monkey went joy riding on a nearby digger and smashed those plaques into oblivion.

The flaw in my Utopian dream though is that there isn't anywhere to get drunk within a mile of here, so for supporters who are thirstier than I am the only thing missing from this 'football by footpath' entry is a pub, and I somehow doubt the beautiful new Mormon chapel on nearby Westside Close (pictured on the opposite page) is going to offer you much, despite the courteous 'Visitors Welcome' sign outside. The Mormons actually prefer to be entitled 'The Church of Jesus Christ of Latter-day Saints'. So there you have it. I have. I imagine they also prefer people don't accidentally leave the second 'm' out of their nickname, as I almost (accidentally) did.

Anyway, I have digressed, the short cut is via the third cul-de-sac to your left, Bunting Lane, and through a gap in the hedgey fencey thing. The away end then slaps you in the face like a wet turbot.

If you take the short cut you will however miss the traditional entrance into the stadium. So for the more conventional of you, walk West along the Portway and then turn right into Partridge Way.

As you approach the entrance to the Ray Mac it not only reinforces my feeling that many football fans are strangely obsessed with paying money to park inside crowded club car parks, but also that all over the country we have three little words that help to explain why we are so deficient at football at a national level. When I've lived and travelled in Africa kids are playing football everywhere; literally anywhere, including rubbish tips, airport car parks and flat rooftops [hmmm, be careful when sprinting down 'the wing' young 'un].

Football is a unique and truly world-wide sport precisely because at its most basic level it needs no real equipment (a jumble of rags inside an old sock is the African predilection), no real pitch, no real organisation, and can be practised with virtually any number of players, including alone, dribbling around old tin cans, nutmegging local mutts, and being sharp enough to make sure your sock ball doesn't roll into a rotting sewer. No wonder the skill and balance levels there are often astonishing.

So what does our society do to encourage our kids to have an off the cuff knockabout? We stick up those three petty words that split apart communities nation-wide; 'No Ball Games'. The new-ish housing estate outside the Ray Mac had not only the largest such sign I've ever seen, but was bolted incongruously onto the side of a house and had the additional warning of 'Strictly' added beforehand, with <u>underlining</u> (pictured below). I'm surprised it wasn't done in **bold** and CAPITALS as well, and have locals enforce the rule with a Tazer.

The ubiquitous satellite dish next to it was allowed though, suggesting we are a nation happy to watch football on TV, but we daren't let our kids play it near our house. And all this was within 20 metres of a football stadium, where they also wouldn't be allowed to play without a rather middle-class appointment. Can I use the word irony for this state of affairs, or will the QI team tell me off?

Rovers won a really good game with four excellent goals and we were treated to the truly bizarre sight of a 1930's bi-plane flying over the ground as if the spirit of Baron van Richthofen or René Fonck were still alive.

This 'football by footpath' route is only a stunted walk (maybe 12-15 minutes the short route, and 15-20 the longer method), but the stroll could be extended if you started your journey in the Hampton Park area of North Salisbury and utilised the full length of Green Lane. Notices by the airfield announce that a massive new planning application is going into Wiltshire Council with an aim to redevelop the whole area, including the building of 480 new houses, so god knows what the area may look like in years to come. So, get your 'football by footpath' mini-adventure in quick before Mr Wimpey does.

* ——————————————————————————— *

**'football by footpath'** is my occasional blog to chart away day travels to British football grounds that use any slightly quirky method of arrival. This will usually involve a smidgen of research, a public footpath or a canal towpath, shanks' pony, a pub and preferably decent weather.

*Why am I happy to arrive at the back entrance via an overgrown field full of cow pats?*

Well, I like thinking outside the box, or even ripping the whole box up and starting again. And as much as I love a packed football terrace INSIDE the ground, don't you sometimes prefer to avoid the modern day madding crowd outside of it and not be herded along some tedious route for away fans? There is also the bonus of being in the great British countryside, free parking or a less than obvious train station, an easier getaway, being greener, and hopefully a country pub that isn't full of sweaty Ipswich Town fans.

# the year of Ludd

## published on Wednesday 5th August 2015

---

### *Saturday 25th July - 7th Pre-season Friendly*

### Cheltenham Town 2    Bristol Rovers 1

Waters - 7' & 40'    Lockyer - 10'

**Rovers:** Mildenhall, Lockyer, J. Clarke, Parkes, Greenslade (Leadbitter - 46'), Gosling, Lines, O. Clarke (Bodin - 65'), Montaño (Sinclair - 46'), Blissett (Taylor - 46'), Harrison.

Attendance: 1,100 inc 317 Gasheads.   Referee: Mark Pottage

---

### *Friday 31st July - 8th Pre-season Friendly & Testimonial Match for Phil Kite*

### Bristol Rovers 0    West Bromwich Albion 4

Sir Rickie of Lambert - 23' & 47', Gardner - 34', Anichebe - 78'

**Rovers:** Mildenhall, Leadbitter, J. Clarke, Parkes, Lockyer, Gosling (O. Clarke - 62'), Sinclair, Lines, Bodin (Montaño - 45'), Taylor, Harrison (Easter - 28').

*Unused Substitutes:* Preston, Lucas, Blissett, Greenslade.

Attendance: 4,068 inc 308 Throstles.   Referee: Lee Probert

---

### ⊗ In recent Rovers news ⊗

☠ The BIG news finally breaks.  Darrell Clarke agrees a new contract. He isn't a naughty boy, he really is the messiah.

☠ Billy Bodin stays via a short-term deal after playing a considerable part in six out of the eight pre-season friendlies.

☠ Winger Jeffrey Monakana signs on a month-long loan from Brighton & Hove Albion.

I have to slightly apologise in advance for my Rovers articles this coming season, as they may not be quite as up-to-date as before, nor blessed with as much information of what might be going on at a modern football club.

This is because I'm doing an experiment for the coming season, where I take the life of a football supporter back-to-basics, without the Internet and all the corresponding trappings that are associated with football forums, twitter gossip, and 24-hour rolling news coverage.

When I became a Gashead in 1989 we gleaned our information from a variety of sources, mainly from media output such as the match day programme, the Bath Chronicle, the Bristol Evening Post, local radio, Ceefax / Teletext, and the infamous premium rate 0898 Club Call telephone service (not that I ever used it). We also had more personal and serendipitous sources; your mates, the stranger next to you on the terrace who relentlessly held a tiny radio up to his ear, overhearing gossip in the pub or on the bus, and even the chatter of the turnstile operator on your way into Twerton.

They were innocent times, when I often knew very little about the team I was about to watch, and certainly didn't have a handle on the intricacies of player contracts, their personal lives, the latest training ground bust ups, or rumours about potential new players, and often didn't even know matters as basic as the state of our injury list.

Whilst the quality of our sources may have been excellent, the length and breadth of them wasn't. I will always remember the delight of promotion in May 1990 as it meant we gained a hallowed spot on the Ceefax network, with a guaranteed page of our own for every match report (about 130 words), without having to be squeezed onto a 'Division Three round up' page.

This experiment is NOT a nostalgia trip though. I'm not saying it was better when we weren't bombarded with information, and everyone had an opinion about EVERYTHING in life - yes, I realise the words pot, kettle and black could be rearranged at this point...

No, this is simply a back to basics jaunt, without any judgement or knee jerk 'modern life is rubbish' type crusade. It's just as much a time-saving exercise for me, as knowing too much about the football club you support is very time consuming indeed. I'm not anti-technology, but then again nor were the much maligned Luddites. They were worried more about rapid over-reliance on labour-saving devices in their workplace rather than the talented inventors themselves. They smashed machines, not people.

I used to live in Lancashire, not a million miles from Burton's Mill in Middleton where the British Army fought a pitched battle with thousands of local workers in April 1812. And on forays across the border into West Yorkshire I loved visiting the absorbing town of Marsden, which arguably became the centre of attention for the entire struggle, although in true football fan style they blamed the louts at Longroyd Bridge in Huddersfield as the real trouble makers!

The intriguing graves of James and Enoch Taylor lie next to the town stocks, and commemorate the brotherly smithies who invented a cropping machine. Although they were quite average local working men, their creativity caused a problem as it did the work of ten hand croppers. They also made sledge-hammers, entitled 'Enochs', which gave rise to the irony of their sledgehammers being used to smash factory machines, and a taunt the Luddites used - 'Enoch made 'em, Enoch shall break 'em'.

The real crux of Luddism though was borne out by the fact that whilst the Taylor's were never vilified, the mill owners who brought in the new machines with indecent haste were, and Marsden made national news when local mill owner William Horsfall, who had barricaded and fortified his Ottiwell's Mill, was ambushed and murdered by a trio of thugs in nearby Crosland Moor.

Their trial at York Castle in 1813, alongside 60 other so-called Luddites, was more of a 'show trial' to petrify the working class into a stony acquiescence than true justice for each individual defendant. 15 men were executed and Luddite style acts petered out.

So there you have it, I'm going to try to keep my football fandom simple this season, but still passionate, and if I accidentally slip in names like Warboys, Bamford and Tillson, don't blame me, blame the clicking and whirling of the printing presses, trying to catch up to modern life.

# a fresh challenge

## published on Friday 7th August 2015

⊗   **In recent Rovers news**   ⊗

Jamie Lucas goes out on a months loan to National League newcomers Boreham Wood. The National League is the nonsensical new name for the top two tiers of non-league football, even though the second tier is not national. The Football Conference is now entitled the National League, and Conference North and Conference South are oxy-moronically entitled National League North and National League South.

Confused? You should be.

What can Gasheads expect from a season back in League Two? Personally I anticipate more of the same, with a tight-knit team improving as the season goes on, and staggered signings and loanee's coming and going to fill gaps. My heart says we could well continue our upward momentum, as many teams have done in the past, but my head reminds me that in nine previous seasons in 'the easiest League in the world to get out of' we had August optimism every season but reached the play-offs just once, and only finished in the top half of the table two other years, and they were both a statistic scrapping 12th. If a cheeky wag had made a T-shirt emblazoned with the slogan, 'Bristol Rovers - Lowering Expectations since the 20th Century', we couldn't really have feigned indignation at it.

Although I'm obviously still elated at our swift exit from non-league, the reality is that for most of the 21st Century I have been shaking my head when I comprehend what division we're playing in. They can rename it as many times as they like ('Third Division', 'League Two') but if you put lipstick on a pig it's still a pig. We all know it's the Fourth Division, and when inelegantly trying to explain it to a non-football fan I often find myself lapsing into that dreaded phrase, 'the bottom division'; a division we had always successfully evaded.

For more than four decades since the creation of the Fourth Division in 1958 Rovers cemented their quirky position of being the last remaining club to have never experienced the highs or lows of either the top or the bottom divisions of the Football League. Whilst that lot south of the river lived their decadent footballing life like Ian Ogilvy dressed in a white suit and recreating the Russian roulette scene from 'The Deer Hunter', we ploughed a somewhat dull, but maybe under appreciated, middle ground.

All that ended in 2001 with the meltdown of Ian Holloway, and the patented first AND second 'worst decisions ever made... ever™', when giving the rescue job to Garry Thompson, who would look out of depth even in a toddlers paddling pool, and managed a deplorable 49 points from 43 League games in two separate spells.

Yes, that's not a typo, he was given another crack at it despite relegation at his first attempt, and would have achieved a landmark double relegation if it wasn't for a Halifax Town charlatan XI masquerading as a football team and the glory days of only one horrifying team being relegated into non-league. How exactly did that all happen? Let's just not go there, eh...

Statistically there is good news for our forthcoming season. Analysis of the first year performances of teams that have been promoted from the Conference since two clubs have gone up (2002/03) shows, well... that quite frankly just about everything is possible except instant relegation.

So, for those worried about being drawn into a relegation dogfight the average placing of newbies like us is greatly comforting. The Conference champions have finished their fresher year in League Two occupying an average position of 12th, with 64 points, whilst the Conference play-off winners are neatly just a smidgen behind, in an average position of 13th, with 62 points.

This does somewhat hide an important detail though; namely that only in a golden period of four seasons in a row from 2005 to 2009 has the play-off winner ever finished above the champion. Since then it has all been downhill, with only one of the last six Conference play-off winners even crawling into the top half (twelfth!), so recent history suggests we may need to hope for Barnet finishing in the top three so we can tag along into the play-offs.

My desperation to reach that hallowed ground is because seemingly nothing can go wrong if you do manage to reach the top seven in your first season in League Two. Four of the teams that have done so since 2003 have gone straight up to League One via the automatic promotion places and the only team to have finished in the play-offs went on to win at Wembley (Stevenage in 2011, who incidentally are the only team in the Division we have never played before, in League or Cup, as we oddly always seem to be passing like ships in the night, going up and down divisions at the same time).

What does tend to happen though is that clubs on a stratospheric rise find themselves back down to earth about three years later; four of those five instant promotees are now back playing with Football League dregs this season.

More good news is held by the fact that no promoted team has suffered an immediate relegation. Let's hope we don't see that as a record made to be broken. Several promotees have flirted with relegation but the worst League position has been Shrewsbury Town's lowly 21st in 2005, with a joint-record low of 49 points. And, in general, the survival rate over the years is very good. Only five of the last 24 promoted clubs have since been relegated back to non-league.

Let's be Bert Tann's Pirates this season, rather that Ray Graydon's Gas.

### ⊗  Statto Alert - An Ever Present Special  ⊗

Lee Brown was one of only two players who played every minute of the League Two season. The other was Adam Smith, Northampton Town's goal-keeper [or as my little kids amusingly say 'a goaler'], which makes Lee's pitch time even more remarkable. Lee also did the same in all four of our cup games, so was on the pitch for our entire season.

To be fair there were others who would have joined the exclusive club if it wasn't for some unfortunate circumstances. Going into the last game of the season two more players could have achieved it, but Bobby Olejnik of Exeter City (a goalkeeper though…boo) missed the final match for 'personal reasons', and Enda Stevens (Portsmouth's trusty left back) was put on the bench for their dead rubber against the Cobblers, presumably to give him a rest before the play-offs less than a week later.

Connor Roberts played every minute of 45 League games for Yeovil Town, whilst on loan from Swansea City, but missed a game to earn his first Wales Under-21 cap. Connor later signed on loan for the Gas in August 2016 and came with glowing references from Glovers fans.

# the season starts in September?
## published on Friday 14th August 2015

### Saturday 8th August - League Two

## Bristol Rovers 0   Northampton Town 1

O'Toole - 49' [ it just had to be him... ]

**Rovers:** Mildenhall, Leadbitter, J Clarke, Lockyer, Parkes, Brown, Sinclair [Booked], Lines, Montaño (Monakana - 60'), Taylor (Bodin - 71'), Easter (Harrison - 56').

*Unused Substitutes:* Preston, O Clarke, Gosling, Blissett.

Attendance: 8,712 inc 574 Cobblers

Referee: Mark Heywood

---

### Tuesday 11th August - Football League Cup 1st Round

## Bristol Rovers 1   Birmingham City 2

Harrison - 65'     Maghoma - 57', Shinnie - 68'

**Rovers:** Mildenhall, Leadbitter, J Clarke (Broom - 81'), Lockyer, Parkes, Brown, Sinclair, O Clarke, Gosling (Montaño - 64'), Harrison, Easter (Taylor - 64').

*Unused Substitutes:* Preston, Blissett, Bodin, Malpas.

Attendance: 5,650 inc 1,150 Bluenoses

Referee: Andy Davies

---

### ⊗  In recent Rovers news  ⊗

☠ Newsflash - Rovers lose opening game of the season and then suffer gallant loss to bigger club in League Cup First Round.

☠ Top animal experts confirm that bears do indeed poo in the woods.

☠ DC has already seen enough of Steve Mildenhall and signs Chesterfield goalkeeper Aaron Chapman on a month-long loan.

Last week I gave an outline of what Gasheads might expect from a season back in League Two. Sadly I didn't have space to add that it is traditional to have a poor opening game, pluckily lose in the First Round of the League Cup to a Championship team, and then see the Mem gate drop by at least 1,000 souls a fortnight later.

I'm not suggesting that Gasheads are fickle, more that there is something about the first home game of a season that brings many casuals and friends to the game, and that the poor performances usually witnessed can hardly encourage them to return quickly. Rovers always seem to be slow starters; in seasons and in each individual game. Maybe it's a rare downside of the laid back Bristolian culture most of us know and love?

In the last 11 seasons we've only won one of our opening fixtures, Paul Buckle's first ever game as manager in August 2012. It was beamed around the world by Sky to capture AFC Wimbledon's first game in the Football League. The AFC incarnation are generally considered to be the spiritual successors of the famed 1889 club who rocked the football world with an FA Cup win in 1988, and 14 consecutive top division seasons despite only being elected to the Football League in 1977. Kevin Keegan would have been proud of the pulsating 3-2 ping-pong match and the utter inability to defend.

Last season's no-score draw opener to Grimsby Town turned out to be a decent result in the long run, and the 7,019 gate was higher than every match in League Two and half the matches in League One, despite being live on TV. This Saturday's loss to Northampton Town attracted 8,712 and was beaten by only two crowds in League One and League Two. I would wager that less than a handful of League Two crowds (bar Portsmouth of course) will top that this entire season.

The crowd against the Mariners was actually our lowest opening day home gate since the famed August 1996 match against Peterborough United which was supposed to be our first ever game at the Memorial Ground, but ended up as our last ever home contest at Twerton Park.

Our average gate for the five opening day home matches since 2004 has been 7,842, and the average of all our last dozen first home League matches of the season, which include three Tuesday night matches, is still an impressive 7,393. The problem though is that the average turnout for the second home League match since 2004 is only 5,918, and that included two bumper crowds against Nottingham Forest (2007) and Southampton (2010 - yes, the game where Saints manager Alan Pardew was sacked afterwards for only murdering us 4-0; meanwhile Rovers shipped in 16 goals in their five games in August).

No-one, literally no-one, can remember the 2-1 loss at Exeter United in August 2013 (Shaquille Hunter came on as sub - enough said); the tame home loss to Oxford United in 2012 was the first of many nails in Mark McGhee's coffin; a 3-0 execution by the Posh at London Road in 2010 gave us an immediate sense of foreboding in what became a relegation season; Leyton Orient said 'thank you very much' in 2009 after taking home a 2-1 win despite Rickie Lambert's goal in his last appearance for Rovers; Carlisle United put three past Steve Phillips in 2008 during a 3-2 win; Andy Williams scored on his debut to rescue a 1-1 draw at Vale Park in 2007; the Posh thrashed us 4-1 in Northamptonshire in 2006, yet we were promoted that season, suggesting that losing to them on first day never leads to a dull season; and Junior Agogo scored against his old club in 2005 to earn us a 1-1 draw at Barnet's quaint old Underhill ground.

So that's one win, three draws, and seven opening day losses since 2005.

I often take solace in life though from knowing that there is always someone worse off than you. Our record is positively superlative compared to that of my best friend's team, Norwich City. No opening day win since 2002, and even that was against a Grimsby Town team who ended up bottom that season whilst plummeting from the Championship to the Conference in a mere eight seasons.

And literally EVERYONE on the planet remembers that 7-1 mauling at Carrow Road in August 2009 to neighbouring minnows Colchester United in their first match back in the third tier for half a century. One brave (or foolhardy?) fan threw his brand new season ticket at Bryan Gunn and harrumphed off in a petulant fit not seen since Bonnie Langford's "I'll scream and scream until I'm sick...and I can!" outbursts in Just William.

The Canaries went on to win the League that season though, so there is clearly no need for panic in our ranks yet.

The First Round of the League Cup shows a similar story, with seven loses in the past 11 outings, five of them 'plucky' defeats to a Championship team. In fact we haven't beaten a team in the same division as us or higher, during normal play since beating newly promoted Brighton & Hove Albion in 2004, courtesy of Lee Thorpe's first Gas cup goal and a pirate poach from Richard Walker on his first Rovers start.

There were real signs of life in the performance against Birmingham City though, and a boisterous atmosphere on the terraces. The lopsided wing-back system didn't seem to click in the first half, as no-one seemed to spot Daniel Leadbitter hugging the touchline, getting lost against the advertising hoardings. It seemed to become a true 3-5-2 formation after the oranges, although the more extroverted we got the more vulnerable we became at the back. Our near misses were eventually punished by a team who seemed to exemplify several aspects of modern football better than we did.

Last season I remarked in this column how tall Rovers were, with several traditionally 'small' positions regularly filled by Tom Lockyer, Lee Brown, Daniel Leadbitter and Andy Monkhouse, all six footers. These days you can maybe get away with a couple of very talented little un's on the pitch but that's about it. Ditto ball-players.

Successful modern teams can just about carry a brace of players whose feet are merely there to keep them standing upright and to clog a ball up to a target man precisely every 97 seconds, but apart from the odd old-school centre-back, a crunch tackling central midfielder, and a shambling target man perhaps, they just cannot be tolerated if you want to get higher up the leagues. Most League Two teams won't have enough of them, including us, although I was impressed by the comfort that new signing James Clarke showed on the ball.

When Tyrone Mings moved to the Premier League for £8m after only 49 professional starts, it must have given heart to any ungainly wide player out there who looks like a horse who has mistaken a football pitch for its paddock.

Welcome to modern football, where you are expected to defend, win headers, go on galloping runs, score goals, be strong, yet light, possess afterburners and carry a 6' 3" frame around ... all at the same time.

# the elephant in the park

## published on Tuesday 18th August 2015

*Saturday 15th August - League Two*

### Yeovil Town 0    Bristol Rovers 1

Harrison - 88'

**Rovers:** Chapman, Leadbitter, J Clarke, Lockyer (Montaño - 75'), Parkes, Brown, Sinclair, Lines, O Clarke (Monakana - 75'), Taylor (Easter - 67'), Harrison.

*Unused Substitutes:* Preston, Gosling, Bodin, Malpas.

Attendance: 5,895 inc 2,038 Gasheads

Referee: Brendan Malone

---

### ⊗  In recent Rovers news  ⊗

☠ Young midfielders Ryan Broom and Dominic Thomas both go out on one month loans, to Taunton Town and Paulton Rovers respectively.

☠ Nathan Blissett returns to the Conference with a month long loan at Tranmere Rovers. He says there is no need to be upset.

---

What better way to celebrate avoiding the deluges affecting other parts of the country than taking a sunny trip into the deepest darkest depression of Somerset, and coming home with our league and play-off unbeaten away run intact (22 games now). If we can hurdle the Hatters and Orient the run will have lasted a whole year.

Over 2,000 fellow Gasheads made the jaunt although only a handful made it via a rural inn and a stroll down a country lane past a 14th Century church in the intriguingly named hamlet of Thorne Coffin. The full story of my idiosyncratic entrance to Huish Park is available as one of my side projects - www.footballbyfootpath.blogspot.co.uk *[Author's note - It is reprinted on the following pages - Oh, lucky you]*

If there had been cries of 'bring out your dead', then at least half the Yeovil Town team would have qualified. As my mate opined, the bottom line about pre-season is that you get players fit. Becoming tactical geniuses at the same time is merely a bonus. Yeovil haven't even managed to produce a fit, injury free team, whereas we mainly have.

Whilst Yeovil were utterly woeful, unfit, and loaded with enormous donkeys front and back, Rovers need to be given credit for sticking to their task, mainly trying to pass the ball around, being adaptable to change, and showing far more desire than the Glovers.

We need to keep our feet on the ground though. This was a vital win precisely because by the end of the season we could well be looking back and thinking 'wow, Yeovil were a dis-jointed and poor team'.

Exactly six years ago, at our first away game of the 2009/10 season, I watched in blazing sunshine at Stockport County, actually feeling sorry for the Hatters after going 2-0 up within eight minutes and fearing a cricket score. Little did we know that a proud and decent local team like County would get relegated from League One that season with a shameful 25 points, and be wallowing in the sixth tier just three years later.

In November 2006 Steve Mildenhall was lining up for the Glovers in their 2-1 victory over Bristol City at a sold out Huish Park. He went on to be their Player of the Season and feature in their gutsy League One Play-Off Final loss to Blackpool.

On a warm day in August 2015 though he was nowhere to be seen.

I am actually glad that the 'elephant in the room' is finally out of the cramped dressing room and bustling through the beautiful Somerset countryside, even if the timing of the end game is not ideal and some people have criticised Darrell Clarke for his unequivocal position. I hope we can attract an affordable keeper to be one of the first names on the team sheet, and I would prefer DC to do it now, rather than later in the season when the transfer window is closed and several points may have already been lost.

Last season (in the fifth tier) Steve Mildenhall did not inspire any confidence except for his shot stopping, which was admittedly the quality of several divisions above his then station. However, that part of a goalkeeper's role is the most straightforward. The more difficult elements are decision making, aerial prowess, commanding an area, and distribution, and I did not see anything last season to suggest that he would be an adequate number one in League Two. And as much as I like Will Puddy, especially his distribution and confident attempts to command his area, he does not have the stature or strength to be a regular number one at this level or higher.

Personally I would have loved it if we could have allowed both of them to leave, and spent the money on one exceptional keeper and a promising, cheap, understudy. Unfortunately the fly in the ointment had already nose-dived into the calamine lotion, as a one year contract extension, constructed when the king of dubious contracts, John Ward, was in charge, had already kicked in about two-thirds of the way through the season.

Contrary to popular rumour this did not happen at the end of the season in April, or even with his Tim Krul-esque appearance at Wembley for the penalty shoot-out. The fact that Puddy was favoured over Mildy after his weak display at the Shay in mid-March, despite the contract extension already having kicked in, spoke volumes.

There are two types of exacting managers; those who are strict and cruel, and those who are strict and fair. I see Darrell Clarke as the latter. He hasn't verbally disparaged Mildy, childishly frozen him out, or told the press before talking to the man himself. He has given Mildy the courtesy of a final look and then conclusively decided, as many of us terrace dwellers already had, that he is not the right man to take us any further.

I don't see how that is in any way disrespectful to a player who we pay very adequately to be a number one goalkeeper and is simply not performing well enough. And talk of treating him better because he's been a good servant to the club for two and a half years rather dishonours Billy Clark, Stuart Campbell, Vaughan Jones, Andy Tillson and many others before my time who gave much of their career to Rovers.

When deciding to change keepers I do have to add one caveat though, namely that goalies can blow hot and cold, just like wingers. Man of the Match Glovers keeper Artur Krysiak is the same Artur Krysiak who was being scouted by Billy Smart's Circus every time we used to play Exeter City.

Go figure.

# special feature
# football by footpath

## Yeovil Town F.C. vs. Bristol Rovers F.C.

### League Two - 15th August 2015

What better way to celebrate avoiding the deluges affecting other parts of the country than taking a sunny trip into the deepest darkest depression of Somerset.

I have always been suspicious of Yeovil and indeed have never bothered to visit the town in any guise; not even Huish Park, amidst the delightful trading estate that surrounds it, despite it sometimes being one of my closest away days. My suspicion is based purely on looking at a map of Somerset and feeling that somehow Yeovil, like Sherbourne, belongs in Dorset.

And if it belongs there, then it must be a cuckoo in the nest of the land of skull cracking cider, coastal mud, amazing music, and tales of Avalon; a Quisling of the West Country; a low down, sneaky, whistle blowing, snake in the grass.

Yeovil strikes me as the kind of shifty place that makes its own moonshine, marries off pigs in nocturnal sky clad ceremonies, and could well wake up one day and unilaterally decide to declare independence, or become a Rutland style state, dwarfed by its more serious neighbouring counties. It's just not right to be forced to witness this underbelly on the map of Somerset, like a fat man dragging his testicles and semi-liquid paunch along a floor. Its quite unbecoming of a proud county, one that my father almost died for in Cyprus.

Even though I love Somerset, the county I was born in (or was I? Avon and Wiltshire complicate things; don't ask, all I can say is that I've had an identity crisis ever since entering this cruel world), and could quite happily hug a stranger from Portishead, Watchet, Shepton Mallet, or even the wonderfully entitled Marston Bigot, I've never felt any attachment to Yeovil at all. And although I won't trot out the tired and rather condescending cliché of Yeovil not being a place of any particular interest, it is a simple fact that whilst Yeovil has three buildings with Grade I listed status, the City I spent most of my youth in, Bath, has over 600 such exceptional structures. Yes, 600.

I am slightly reminded at this point of a certain incident around 2,000 years ago. Readers who went to Sunday School may recognise the following passage from John's Gospel [ch 1, verse 43-46], albeit with a few geographical amendments. "The next day he [Jesus] wanted to leave for Clifton. Jesus then found Philip and said to him: "Be my follower." Now Philip was from Bath, from the city of Andrew and Peter. Philip found Nathanael and said to him: "We have found the one of whom Moses, in the Law, and the Prophets wrote: Jesus, the son of Joseph, from Yeovil." But Nathanael said to him: "Can anything good come out of Yeovil?". Philip said to him: "Come and see." "

My admittedly jaundiced and intolerant assumptions of Yeovil probably weren't helped by by-passing it as a kid. I have fond 'memories' of Minehead, where I won 'Best Baby' at Butlins in the early 70's (I suspect it was a walkover, and that my parents had accidentally booked us in for the over-60's week). I can still feel love for Cheddar Gorge, despite the tourist tat, and have memories of adequate days out at Weston-Super-Mud, amidst swathes of Brummies. I have climbed up Glastonbury Tor, yomped on Exmoor, and had a wazz at Taunton Deane services. But Montacute House is the closest I've ever been to Yeovil.

I also hold Shepton Mallet in high esteem, mainly for many happy days at agricultural shows at the nearby Bath & West Showground, but also for the free gift that kept on giving; the drive past the Jeff Koons-esque Babycham fawn (pictured above) that seemed to jump and prance from the roof of the Showerings factory as the car rattled its way down the hill into the Mallet. And how could I almost overlook bouncing on beds at the J.R.Haskins showroom, THE place to go before Ikea ripped up Eastville, imposed their cultural hegemony on a proud nation built by Mr. Chippendale (no, not those Chippendales!) and crushed the humble furniture retailers of Britain in their massive Viking hands like a moderately portly man sitting on one of their dreadful £6 chip wood triangular side tables (probably called 'Bumtings' or 'Fartburst') painted in an oh-so wacky colour that gets your wife's pretentious friends talking as they stick their obnoxious noses in the bottle of Farm Foods Irish Wine that you told them was a Waitrose Zinfandel - God knows how they got the cat to sit on that bottle. They couldn't tell the difference, but I bet they think they could.

But Yeovil was always bypassed, until today. Any journeys beyond the Shepton Mallet area were invariably heading for the South Coast, and there was definitely no reason to stop on the way towards leaping into the sea, sand and sunshine of Weymouth and Bournemouth, both proper Dorset destinations. Yeovil existed in this twilight zone of nothingness, betwixt and between. Even Albert Camus and J.M.Coetzee would find it impossible to find any existence there at all.

My 'football by footpath' mini adventure starts from The Carpenters Arms (web - http://carpenters-chilthorne.co.uk ) on the edge of Chilthorne Domer, at the crossroads of the wonderfully entitled Vagg Lane and Tintinhull Road. The official postcode is BA21 3PX, but if you're a satnaver try BA21 3PY, which actually drops you closer to it. It's just one mile from Huish Park and avoids the traffic / parking and lack of pubs that Pirates always protest about. If you prefer double the walk you could start at the more prominent Halfway House Inn, on the A37 itself (Illchester Road, BA22 8RE- www.halfwayhotelyeovil.com ) which lets you sample the delights of a walk through Chilthorne Domer village itself - more of that later.

The Carpenters Arms has an adequate car park, adequate beer, adequate food, above adequate staff and describes itself as "...sympathetically restored and modernised..."; you mean made to look like every other airy but bland restoration job, more akin to a Jif commercial than somewhere to feel truly at home. Molson Coors' Doom Bar (only partly from Cornwall these days) seems to be the regular ale, with a guest on the other pump. Today it was a rather cloudy, and slightly sour Glastonbury Hedge Monkey, which according to its maker, is "Brewed in honour of Glastonbury's many free-spirited cosmic visitors (hippies in other words!)". I wonder how the French say cliché?

The 20 minute walk to the ground is straight down a single country lane, so getting lost is virtually impossible, and as the lane is a no-through road, it's more akin to a private path, with probably one tractor a day, a few cars per week and a young herd of Holstein Friesian's (pictured left) occasionally being moved around. The lane passes through the gorgeous hamlet of Thorne Coffin, with various curiosities to arouse the inquisitiveness of polymaths like myself, and presumably a great place to film a zombie slasher epic?

There is a herringbone stone wall the likes of which I've never quite seen before, a Jubilee Hall which looks more like it should be on a Dorset beach, and the stunning Thorne House (photos of both on the opposite page), which could almost pass for an Elizabethan Manor House if it hadn't actually been built in 1882, by Sir Thomas Graham Jackson one of the most distinguished architects and scholars of his day. He is remembered mostly for numerous work in Oxford, including the 'Bridge of Sighs' that joins two parts of Hertford College over New College Lane.

The barely visible clock tower suggests there is a stable block behind, and the incongruous 'Conference' sign (below left) was thankfully pointing away from Huish Park! There is no way we want to be going in that direction ever again.

Finally the tiny 14th Century 'Church of St. Andrew', a grade II* listed building, is worth a quick gander, with a charming North porch dated to 1613 (above right).

As this lane finishes, walk straight over the road, down a path and you are suddenly into the Trading Estate where Huish Park lies. They even handily put the away end at the North end, just for us football by footpathers.

There isn't much to say about the ground. I don't mean that in a bad way; it's just that we went to a football match, and then left afterwards. That's about it really, except for the curious sight that greeted me in the toilets, and the wry comment of a fellow visitor who mused "Hmmm...maybe we need some more paper towels?" (pictured below). Oh, and when hurriedly entering the ground I'm convinced a steward asked

if I had "any spices or bottles", as if cinnamon sticks and massive nutmegs had recently become the sophisticated hooligans' weapon of choice, mirroring the ubiquitous rise of pulled pork in a brioche roll, all served by some beard-ed, inked up spanner, necking a craft beer or a flat white.

The game was... well, adequate. A 'Please Do Not Climb On The Walls' sign seen later in the day, at Nunney Castle, would have been better off nailed to the away end, as us Gasheads were slightly climbing the walls wondering if we would ever get one past Artur Krysiak; yes, the very same Artur Krysiak who was being scouted by Billy Smart's Circus every time we used to play Exeter City. Go figure.

If there had been cries of 'bring out your dead', then at least half the Yeovil Town team would have qualified. As my mate opined, the bottom line about pre-season is that you get players fit. Becoming tactical geniuses at the same time is merely a bonus. Yeovil haven't even managed to produce a fit team, whereas we mainly have. Glovers fans must be extremely worried at three losses on the trot, no goals, and the spectre of a triple relegation. Hopefully Dan Cabell, the febrile Glovers fan who held up a distinctly home made sign live on TV just over a year ago, stating 'Could be worse we could support Bristol Rovers #non-league', will have kept his Magnus Opus and with a few amendments can be shown the error of his ways later this season.

Whilst Yeovil were utterly woeful, unfit, and loaded with enormous donkeys front and back, Rovers need to be given credit for sticking to their task, mainly trying to pass the ball around, adapting to change, and showing far more desire than the Glovers. I lost count of the amount of times The Beard, Ollie Clarke and even Chris Lines nipped into to steal the ball off a Glover, or win the ball back after momentarily losing it. 67% possession, 11 corners and 16 shots (half on target), tell a story of persistence, even if the final decisive ball was often lacking, and the formation seems to be confusing some of our players.

A wander through Chilthorne Domer village afterwards was a bonus although sadly we missed a mid 18th Century six seater privy that was in regular use until 1939. Yes, a privy - an outside toilet, crapper, W.C., bog, loo, stinkpit, oval office, little room, dunny, thunder box, house of ease, latrine, necessarium, long drop, brick s**t house, porcelain throne, lavvy, khazi, poo room, los servicios, the swanie. Call it what you like, it's a Grade II* listed structure, meaning it's in the top 8% of listed buildings and of "more than special interest" in our green and pleasant land.

The similarly Grade II* listed Parish Church of St. Mary the Virgin (pictured left) has 13th century origins and is easily spotted from Main Street (BA22 8RD). It has two beautiful pathways of shaped Yew trees, intriguing gargoyles, and a eye-catching oblong bell turret, which is apparently very similar to the one at the Church of St. Andrew at nearby Brympton D'Evercy, that one being in the illustrious company of only 94 Grade I listed buildings in South Somerset.

The churchyard contains the poignant grave of Piers Simon (see left) who tragically died in the Indian Ocean tsunami on Boxing Day 2004 whilst visiting his brother Luke in Koh Phi Phi, Thailand. His family have set up the Piers Simon Appeal - www.pierssimonappeal.org - in his honour, with the 'School in a Bag' a particularly noteworthy initiative.

The War Memorial (pictured right) by the entrance to the Church Yard includes an inscription for 25 year old Lieutenant Richard Madden of the Light Dragoons who was killed in Bosnia on 28th January 1996, alongside two other Dragoons, when their Spartan combat reconnaissance vehicle hit a mine at Titov Drvar whilst on peacekeeping duties with the Implementation Force (IFOR). Overall 59 UK service personnel died helping to bring peace and stability to Bosnia and Herzegovina.

## Lest we forget

# three is the magic number
## published on friday 28th August 2015

---

### *Tuesday 18th August - League Two*

#### Luton Town  0    Bristol Rovers  1
Sinclair - 90 + 4'

**Rovers:** Chapman, Leadbitter [Booked], J Clarke, Lockyer, Parkes, Brown, Sinclair, Lines, O Clarke, Harrison [Booked], Easter (Taylor - 68').

*Unused Substitutes:* Mildenhall, Gosling, Bodin, Malpas, Montaño, Monakana.

Attendance: 8,061 inc 553 Gasheads

Referee: Trevor Kettle

---

### *Saturday 22nd August - League Two*

#### Bristol Rovers  3    Barnet  1
Brown - 2', Easter - 77', Taylor - 87'    Weston - 85'

**Rovers:** Chapman, Leadbitter (Gosling - 32'), J Clarke, Lockyer [Booked], Parkes, Brown [Booked], Sinclair, Lines, O Clarke, Harrison (Taylor - 60'). Easter (Bodin - 83').

*Unused Substitutes:* Mildenhall, Mansell, Montaño, Monakana.

Attendance: 7,107 inc 199 Bees

Referee: Ross Joyce

---

Daniel Leadbitter has been lauded in this blog many times, and it is a shame that he pulled up lame whilst on a typical gallop down the right flank against Barnet. I rated him the first time I saw him play because whilst touch and tactics can be taught, the pace and height he possesses are not quite so easy. The 3-5-2 formation really suits his strengths, in fact, it really suits all our players at the moment, even if a few are still adapting to it, and it leaves three or four 'proper' wingers sitting on a bench twiddling their thumbs and lacking game time.

I was skeptical of the formation when losing to Birmingham City in the League Cup a fortnight ago, because it seemed more like a 5-3-2 at times, or a lopsided system as Lee Brown couldn't get forward much and no-one seemed to spot Daniel Leadbitter hugging the touchline, getting lost against the advertising hoardings, and no-one passed to him. When three at the back was tried last season it didn't seem to work either, especially when used in a 3-4-3 formation. However, it has certainly worked far better in the last three games.

With Chris Lines and Lee Mansell usually first on the team sheet for central midfield, The Beard's talents can easily be wasted in a 4-4-2 crammed with central midfielders; it either forces him out wide and away from the real action, or can result in a narrow midfield and a lack of crosses into the box.

Whilst we all love Stuart Sinclair and he is never one to complain, in this situation his happy bunny attribute is strangely not helpful. It's very lovely to know that The Beard is happy to play anywhere but he is nowhere near as effective stuck out wide. This new midfield ménage à trois 'solves' this problem, although Darrell Clarke will soon have a new selection headache because Ollie Clarke has put in his best run of Rovers performances just prior to Lee Mansell's return from injury.

The back three are soundly balanced, although it is unexpectedly Tom Parkes, often our outstanding performer, who probably looks the weakest of the triumvirate at the moment. The potency of three at the back is that it still manages to let our trio play pretty much in their own best positions.

Readers of this blog will know that I was not a big fan of Tom Lockyer as an almost permanent fixture at right back last season. He is a very good centre-back, and it's great to finally be able to fit his round peg in a round hole this season. Parkes has been a bit quiet, and maybe a bit heavy, but the role should also suit him, as a left footer and someone who is increasingly comfortable at trying to bring the ball out from the back.

The complete revelation though is James Clarke. What a ball player this man is. A centre-back who was often played at right back by previous managers; the epitome of the modern defender, with a bit of pace, a pass, a willingness to get forward and real comfort on the ball. Not hugely tall, but hardly Prince-like in his stature either. If we want to look upwards we need as many ball players in our team, and currently James Clarke is leading the way.

Finally, the no-brainers of Lee Brown and Daniel Leadbitter as wing-backs. But is it a no brainer?

Lee Brown is easily one of my favourite Rovers' players for many years, but I think he is the one who has slightly struggled with the 3-5-2. Last season he excelled as the conventional over-lapping foil for Andy Monkhouse, often ending up higher up the pitch than his left-sided partner, but safe in the knowledge that Monky would be providing quite an obstacle to get past if the play broke down. The new season must have required a rethink of his brief, although he is already looking more comfortable there now.

Daniel Leadbitter is almost a born wing-back, with gazelle like legs, pace to cover any breaks or youthful mistakes, and a curiosity to want to know what is going on up the other end of the pitch. It comes as no surprise to see him designated as the player left on the centre spot when the others go up for a corner, nor that in his youth he was a promising 400m runner and last February knew more about Gateshead Stadium's athletics track than its football pitch.

The only real issue is the age-old question of whether the understanding of a new system can come quickly enough. Patience is not a well known quality in football and the problem with these complicated new fangled dangled formations is often that it takes a while to bed in, whereas fans, and managers, will often jettison them at the first sign of trouble. That happened to a degree last season, when three at the back was tried, mainly as a 3-4-3, but in that case the swap back to a trusted 4-4-2 was more because we had different, and regularly changing, personnel at the club and DC didn't risk us getting forward a bit more or upsetting the lop-sided left and right wide partnerships that often worked quite well.

A spirited Cup loss to a Championship team, followed by three straight wins whilst only conceding a solitary goal, certainly seems to suggest it is now bedding in well. There will of course be tests to come: maybe a team with pace up front and on the wings; Leadbitter's injury perhaps; or trying to break down a deep defence with little room to manoeuvre, but it is a nice weapon to have in our armoury, and possessing what is usually a Plan B as your Plan A can often prove to be a headache for any opposition.

# do you remember the first time?

### published on Thursday 3rd September 2015

---

*Saturday 29th August - League Two*

## Leyton Orient 2    Bristol Rovers 0

James - 23' (pen), Simpson - 45'

**Rovers:** Chapman, Lyttle (Monakana - 45'), J Clarke, Lockyer, Parkes, Brown, Sinclair, Lines, O Clarke (Montaño - 45'), Easter (Taylor - 61'), Harrison.

*Unused Substitutes:* Mildenhall, Bodin, Gosling, Mansell.

Attendance: 5,777 inc 1,023 Gasheads

Referee: Darren Drysdale

---

⊗    **In recent Rovers news**    ⊗

Loss at League leaders Leyton Orient meant Rovers agonisingly fell just a week short of a going an entire year undefeated in league away games.

---

Jarvis Cocker may well have been singing about something slightly more salacious than kicking a pigs bladder around a grass enclosure, but professional footballers will always tell you that no matter what heights you may rise to you'll never forget your first Football League appearance.

In this truly pathetic era of £200,000 a week football players jetted in from all over the world it is therefore quite special to see your own little club have faith in relatively local non-league finds when giving Matty Taylor, Stuart Sinclair and James Clarke their first career appearances in the Football League, with the first two also already bagging their opening goals.

Nathan Blissett may make his own debut later this season, and although Will Puddy did have one Football League game for fun six years ago, I see him as a soon-to-be debutant really.

With ages ranging from 25 to 27, some of these five may be treading a fine line between genuine late bloomers and players who may never be quite good enough to make that much impact on any of the three Football League divisions, but at least they are getting a deserved chance to show what they are capable of.

We've also just had a promising young 'un make his first professional appearance of any description. Tyler Lyttle impressed me in the first pre-season friendly at Salisbury and it must have been great for him to get a start so early in the season, even if he was the sacrificial lamb in a half-time formation change. Although such a curt debut may knock the confidence a little (no pun intended), it is surely better than having to wait until the obligatory 'kid blooding' ceremony on the final day of the season.

I rather assumed that some of our other younger players had never played at this level either, so whilst doing my research I was surprised to find that our old friend Martin Allen gave Willem Puddy (his mother is Dutch and possibly still awaits his call-up for the Oranje) his one and only League appearance in May 2009 for the final game of Cheltenham Town's worst ever League season. They had already been relegated back to League Two, with a paltry 39 points, hence why Willem was between the sticks for a 2-0 defeat at Southend in front of almost 9,000 baying Shrimpers. Who was the keeper at the other end? Why, none other than Stephen James Mildenhall, presumably when he was enjoying better times.

Others who had a youthful sojourn in the Football League before dropping down to non-league include Jake Gosling and Daniel Leadbitter.

Gozzy, a.k.a. 'eyebrows', made his League debut as a sub for Exeter City in January 2013, and made his starting debut the month later alongside ex-Gas heroes, also-rans and villains; Jamie Cureton, Pat Baldwin and, Danny Coles.

Leads, a.k.a. 'legbitten' for the amount of fouls committed on him when in flight, had a very similar West Country experience in his youth, with a League debut as a sub for Torquay Utd in October 2011, and a first start a year later.

Both had less than 20 League games before being released into a new life elsewhere, so I've also found it very satisfying to see them make their Rovers debuts in the Football League.

We may not have the best team in the world, and we may not even be the best run club in the world, but at least we are trying to give players a chance to live their dream, and to always remember their first time.

# a club who would have me as a member
## published on Thursday 10th September 2015

---

*Sunday 6th September - League Two*

**Bristol Rovers 0     Oxford United 1**

Roofe - 62'

**Rovers:** Chapman, J Clarke (Bodin - 84'), Lockyer, Parkes, Brown, Sinclair, Lines, O Clarke [Dismissed], Mansell (Montaño - 74'), Easter, Taylor (Harrison - 67').

*Unused Substitutes:* Mildenhall, Lyttle, Monakana, Greenslade.

Attendance: 7,038 inc 633 Gasheads

Referee: James Linington

---

This week I would like to introduce the Fan's Forum Sponsor Club (FFSC) to any Gashead who doesn't yet know about them. This innovative idea was set up in early 2013 by Jon Thorne, and promoted to Gasheads on the BRFC Fan's Forum. It has managed to ride the tidal waves of relegation, and emerged even stronger as a simple club for Gasheads who want to trade in positivity, not negativity. In fact I would go so far as to say that it should never be forgotten that when BRFC were at their depths, and not many people wanted to sponsor players or matches in non-league, the FFSC filled an incredibly important gap.

The idea is simple. Members pay just £10 per season, with all proceeds going to support Bristol Rovers. Members not only get a warm fuzzy feeling inside for supporting their club in a fresh way, but also have a statistically excellent chance of winning various 'prizes' given away throughout the season. Since January 2013 it has raised over £13,500 for the club, including paying for the kit sponsorship of 26 players, predominantly youngsters, sponsorship of four first team games, and being a member of the BRFC 1883 Shirt Sponsorship Draw.

The FFSC aims to:

- ✖ Encourage unity and positivity;
- ✖ Raise funds for the football club we all love;
- ✖ Sponsor players who may not normally attract a sponsor;
- ✖ Sponsor home games, plus if possible some youth team games;
- ✖ Offer members reduced prices for selected match hospitality;
- ✖ Meet up with other like-minded Gasheads; and,
- ✖ Last but not least, give away prizes to members, including match worn shirts of players who've been sponsored, and free hospitality places.

Can you imagine how a young player must feel when they read the match day programme and see that nearly all the better known players have been sponsored by various businesses and individuals, but they haven't? And can you now imagine how cherished they must feel when informed that a fans club has decided to sponsor them? That is the unique selling point of the FFSC.

I don't feel that the club is competing with the Supporter's Club because that club has a clearly defined role as a service provider and also has a representational / advocacy role within BRFC. It is also not trying to compete with the excellent work of the Community Department, or any other initiatives.

It is just a group of honest individuals who have no hidden agenda and who want to support the club in a slightly different way to what is already out there and working well.

Joining the Fan's Forum Sponsor Club is simple. Payment can be sent to their PayPal Account (bristolroversffsc@yahoo.co.uk), paid direct into a dedicated FFSC Bank account, or paid in cash by meeting one of the volunteers at a game. Full details can be found on various Rovers online forums, including www.gaschat.co.uk and www.gasheads.org

Membership costs just £10 a season, but there is no limit on multiple memberships if you want a higher chance of winning any give-aways.

Groucho Marx famously wrote that he wouldn't want to belong to any club who would have him as a member, and whilst I would generally subscribe to that maxim, I am honoured to make an exception to the rule and to be one of the early members of one of the best clubs in the world.

Have you joined yet?

# for every action there is an equal and opposite reaction

## published on Tuesday 15th September 2015

---

*Saturday 12th September - League Two*

### Bristol Rovers  0    Accrington Stanley  1

Key - 68'

**Rovers:** Nicholls, J Clarke, Lockyer, Parkes [Booked], Brown, Sinclair, Lines, Mansell (Gosling - 65'), O Clarke (Bodin - 77'), Taylor (Easter - 72'), Harrison.

*Unused Substitutes:* Mildenhall, Lyttle, Kilgour, Montaño.

Attendance: 6,351 inc 48 Milkmen

Referee: Kevin Johnson

---

### ⊗  In recent Rovers news  ⊗

☠ 1st Sept - Adam Drury joins on a non-contract basis. He is a defender.

☠ 7th Sept - Adam Drury has left the building, for 'personal reasons'.

☠ Shirt number 39a is retired in memory of Adam Drury's contribution.

☠ Drury later signs for Grimsby Borough; in the 10th level of the pyramid.

☠ Wigan Athletic goalkeeper Lee Nicholls joins on a three-month loan.

---

Although Gasheads generally wouldn't wish a phoenix club any ill will, I think a lot of us wouldn't have minded if Accrington Stanley (1968) had stayed famous for its role as the derogatory unknown club in a milk advert in the 1980s rather than for earning a new crack at the Football League in 2006 and managing to stay there ever since.

The heady days of our first encounter with them (a 4-0 trashing in December 2006) have long since gone, and since an equally overwhelming 5-1 butchery at the Mem in April 2012, Accy have become a real bogey team for us, winning all five encounters since, including three successive 1-0 wins in Horfield. We've also never won at the Crown Ground in four attempts, and our match there on Tuesday 22nd October 2013 was played in front of precisely 1,101 people, probably the lowest League crowd to watch Rovers since 1927.

Sadly our season is now going as some had feared.  Three home losses out of four is hardly the way to keep your core support behind you and the action of losing historically prompts a reaction; the amount of Gasheads at the League home games has steadily dropped from 8,138 at the season to 6,908 and 6,405 for Barnet and Oxford United respectively, and now to 6,303 for Stanley.

If it weren't for the lure of Portsmouth and Wycombe Wanderers for our next games at the Mem, home crowds would fall further I imagine.  Whilst this situation is not unique or unexpected, it is obviously not helpful, and the tsunami of promotion positivity is now more like a sedate wave of realism. The dearth of creativity and the absence a 'banging them in' striker is hardly fresh news.

Although I've always supported Darrell Clarke, I'm not so naïve as to think there is no such scenario that could test some Gasheads' backing of him.

I used to really take pleasure in watching Nigel Pearson's pensive and frank interviews when romping to the Championship title with Leicester City in 2013/14.  The analysis crawled out of his mouth like an asthmatic snail and became almost the antidote to the usual knee-jerk, testosterone fuelled manager interviews, blaming everyone on the planet except their own team, and certainly not themselves.

But it's easy being calm, and even self-deprecating, when regularly winning. The real test of a man's character is when things are going badly and last season was more like watching the meltdown of a Japanese nuclear reactor, as the slow speech and measured aloofness rapidly became passive aggression and downright bullying.

I will therefore watch with baited breath to see how DC reacts to his own mini-crisis, and I expect that he'll respond to it capably.

Although Darrell faced a crisis during his attempts to stave off relegation in 2014, and during the first seven games of last season, he has managed the team so well since that he hasn't had to respond to a proper mini-crisis for an entire year.  Yes, there were odd events that tested our resolve later last season (losing at home to Bath City in the FA Trophy springs to mind, a March blip with only five points from 12, and even the late draw at Dover Athletic on the penultimate weekend of the season) but there certainly wasn't anything to get us Pirates too flustered.

With seven games now gone this season we have only one point more than last seasons' seemingly apocalyptic start, have scored a miserly five goals (the joint fewest in the division), and most importantly are now on an unwanted three game losing streak.

It is of course hard to judge the quality of the opposition so early in the season. At our first away game of the 2009/10 season I watched in blazing sunshine at Stockport County, actually feeling sorry for the Hatters after we went 2-0 up within eight minutes and feared a cricket score. Little did we know that a proud and decent local team like County would get relegated from League One that season with a shameful 25 points, and be in the sixth tier three years later.

Fast forward six years and it is mildly interesting to see that we have lost to four teams currently above us (the first, eighth, tenth and 11th placed teams) and have only beaten teams far below us (those currently lying 20th, 22nd and 23rd).

We now face two of our potentially hardest games of the season, away at Plymouth Argyle and home to Portsmouth (currently second and third in the table respectively), followed by some bright spark scheduling two of our three longest away trips of the season (Hartlepool United and Morecambe) within five days of each other.

Personally I think this spell of four challenges may galvanise the squad and the manager rather than break them, but it's only a hunch.

If you want a more scientific approach I am hoping that Newton's Third Law of Motion can be applied to football, and that this string of defeats will prompt an equal and opposite reaction from Rovers.

Come on you Blues.

# the late late show

## published on Thursday 24th September 2015

*Saturday 19th September - League Two*

### Plymouth Argyle 1    Bristol Rovers 1

Jervis - 85'    Harrison - 90'+1 (pen)

**Rovers:** Nicholls, J Clarke, Lockyer, Parkes, Brown, Sinclair, Lines, Bodin, Gosling (Montaño - 66'), Taylor (Harrison - 69' [Booked]), Easter (Lucas - 86').

*Unused Substitutes:* Mildenhall, Mansell, O Clarke, McChrystal.

Attendance: 10,633 inc 1,587 Gasheads

Referee: Chris Sarginson

### ⊗  In recent Rovers news  ⊗

Colin Sexstone joins as a non-executive director. Sexstone had famously been a long-term Chief Executive (and latterly Chairman of the Board of Directors) at Bristol C*ty and on Gas forums was referred to by a degrading epithet. Most Rovers fans welcomed him with open arms as their feet were getting twitchy over whether the [then] Board had the strength to navigate the Shamesbury's litigation and deliver the UWE Stadium.

Anyone growing up in the 1980's may just remember the explosion in television that happened during that era, with Channel 4 usually the front runner when bringing us unusual TV, the infamous red triangle films and peculiar foreign sports.

As a curious teen I was happy to watch anything slightly different. The Republic of Ireland didn't even have TV until 1961 and although its flagship talk show 'The Late Late Show' was hardly that exotic it was quirky when compared to the standard fare we were served up by the other three channels.

This was still the era when talk shows were conducted in a regimented fashion by grey haired old men in unpleasant polyester suits and receding hairlines. Gay Byrne was the 'The Late Late Show' presenter for almost 40 years, and taken merely at face value could be seen as the epitome of conservative Ireland.

However, the topics the show tackled were often ground breaking for Irish TV and it was once branded 'a dirty programme that should be abolished altogether'.

It may be the world's second longest-running talk show, but the only moment we all remember from half a century of broadcasting is Boyzone's first ever TV appearance in 1993, involving terrifyingly fast homoerotic gyrations and undertaken before they had even recorded one note of music. Byrne milked it for all it was worth, revelling in proclaiming that they had "no talent whatsoever; they don't sing, they don't write music, they don't play instruments", then winding up the 'performance' by sarcastically telling them, "we look forward to hearing from you when you are famous". More encouragingly the show also gave Sinead O'Connor, U2 and The Strypes their first introduction to TV.

Find it on the RTE archive or YouTube, but be sure you are alone when you watch it. It is that bizarre and you may not be able to explain it to your loved ones.

Rovers' late late shows have not been quite so startling, but let's be honest, if it wasn't for late late goals this season we'd be on three points and in the relegation zone.

Don't get me wrong though, there is nothing improper about goals from 80 minutes and onwards; indeed it is quite the opposite. Late goals show a spirit and a fitness that other teams may not possess. They represent a never-say-die attitude and a vital ability to physically and mentally compete to the final whistle, and the character trait is especially valuable when battering a team like Yeovil Town and coming up against a seemingly impenetrable goalie, yet still managing to keep calm and slot a crucial goal home in the dying stages.

Stuart Sinclair's winner in the fourth minute of added time at his home club, Luton Town, was a genuinely lovely move and owed as much to The Beard's fitness and willingness to run and run as anything else. And as much as I'm on record for hating the 'super sub' label given to Ellis Harrison, yet again he pulled something out of the bag as a sub, and even later in added time could have bagged a winner against Plymouth Argyle.

All of the above is just as valid as an early goal, or the performance of a player who races out of the blocks and then fades. Although it may be anxiety inducing as a fan, it is handy to know that we have a squad who are genuinely capable of giving us some hope until the last whistle.

It is also encouraging to see that this is quite a new trait and something that must have been successfully nurtured behind the scenes. Although we often showed resilience last season, successfully coming back from a deficit seven times, we rarely needed an important late goal, with the only two examples of note this year being the Ellis Harrison's 83rd minute winner to kill off a stubborn Braintree Town outfit in February and the best comeback of the season at the Shay in March, with Lee Brown's fizzer and Ellis Harrison's van Basten-esque goal of the season rescuing a late point on a pitch devoid of grass, but heavy on goals.

Long may the late, late show continue, although if you are reading this Mr. Clarke a couple of early, early shows would also be appreciated by my cardiologist.

# can we play you (away) every week?

### published on Tuesday 6th October 2015

---

*Saturday 26th September - League Two*

## Bristol Rovers  1    Portsmouth  2

Easter - 48'      Evans - 29', Stockley - 71'

**Rovers:**  Nicholls, Leadbitter, J Clarke (Gosling - 45' [Booked]), Lockyer [Booked], Parkes, Brown, Sinclair, O Clarke (Bodin - 45'), Lines [Booked], Harrison, Easter (Taylor - 72').

*Unused Substitutes:*  Mildenhall, Montaño, Mansell, McChrystal.

Attendance: 8,555 inc 1,188 Pompeys

Referee: Jeremy Simpson

---

*Tuesday 29th September - League Two*

## Hartlepool  0    Bristol Rovers  3

Taylor - 32', Bodin - 64', Easter - 78'

**Rovers:**  Nicholls, J Clarke, Lockyer, McChrystal [Booked] (Parkes - 82'), Brown, Sinclair, Mansell, Bodin (O Clarke - 84'), Gosling, Taylor, Easter (Harrison - 79' [Booked]).

*Unused Substitutes:*  Mildenhall, Montaño, Lines, Lucas

Attendance: 3,788 inc 190 Gasheads

Referee: Darren Handley

---

### ⊗   In recent Rovers news   ⊗

After one sub cameo against Plymouth Argyle, Jamie Lucas goes back on loan to Boreham Wood.  A similar scenario happens in November when after returning from London he makes a brief appearance at Southend in the JPT, and then goes back to the Wood again in January for the rest of the season.  In all he gets 24 matches under his belt (including five sub appearances), scoring seven goals.

Just when some Gasheads were about to push the huge red panic button we went on our longest and most bizarrely timed away trip of the season (a Tuesday night for a 573 mile round trip; our 190 fans even got a warm round of applause from the monkey hangers), kept our first clean sheet for seven games, and saw a trio of front-line players actually score. Logic flew out the window four days later as our third longest trip also saw a relatively comfortable win, full of goals from strikers, and the seven goals in those two matches stood in sharp juxtaposition to the same number we managed in our first nine league games.

Make an equation to explain that Mr. Einstein!

Whereas football has moved on, not all fans have, and home advantage (or more likely away disadvantage) seems to mean less than it maybe used to. There's nothing THAT unusual anymore about an disappointing home record and a decent away record, especially in the lower leagues.

Teams travel in more style (often overnight for long distances), may stop for a Friday training session in a facility probably better than their own, dank intimidating grounds are few and far between, and pitches are far more uniform than they used to be; the old nugget of a 'level playing field' has been realised more than ever before, with grassless or sloping pitches rarely seen outside of non-league, or Blackpool FC.

Whilst we thrashed Pools there were six other League Two fixtures going the way of the travelling team, whilst only three home wins were registered, all of which were by top five teams. Saturday was similar, with us being one of six teams to plunder the full three points on the road, whilst only half as many managed to win with their so-called home advantage.

Eleven games into the season may not be statistically overwhelming but 13 clubs, including us, currently have better away records than home, with only eleven preferring to be at home. These stats may just be a blip (last year only four teams had a better away record over the whole League Two season) but for the meantime it seems like there is nothing to fear away, unless you are our adversaries from last season, Barnet, who've lost all six league games when absent from their Hive, plus two out of three in cups.

Lower mid-table may not have been what most Gasheads aspired to a few games ago but we had played five of the top six teams, and although a solitary point against them suggested we may struggle with the better teams this season, it was surely less worrying than if we were losing to the lower and middling teams?

Two victories against middling clubs later and things are looking settled again.

The five changes to the starting XI at Pools seemed to have stopped our rot and although I am usually a fan of considerable regularity in a team, I can appreciate that we haven't been able to be settled this season because we simply haven't been good enough and have few outstanding players. Only Lee Brown and Stuart Sinclair now remain as players who've played every minute for us this season.

Tuesday's performance and result suggested that for a manager accused of 'tinkering' too much maybe Darrell Clarke's constant two or three changes per 'project' had not actually taken the ancient art of tinkering far enough. It seems like a bolder shock of the new was needed, and it was intriguing to see two 'undroppables' on the bench in the frozen North East; Tom Parkes and Chris Lines. Parkes' demotion has certainly been deserved as he has clearly been the weakest link of a stuttering defence this season, and continues to miss numerous chances from set pieces.

One of the most fascinating aspects of being a football fan is seeing how long it takes for a reputation to be built and then seeing how long it takes for fans to stop repeating the cliché once it is no-longer true. This season I have read and heard numerous utterances of the old chestnut that we have 'one of the best defences in the division'. We don't. This adage has stuck to us like glue for several seasons now and although it was generally true in the fifth tier, it wasn't really true in our relegation season and it hasn't been true this season. Pompey may be a decent team but the defending for their brace was truly amateurish, and the first two at the Shrimpers were dreadful in the extreme.

Apologists of our relegation season in 2013/14 pointed to the joint tenth best defence in the league, but it's not much of an achievement when your team is back loaded and lacks the creativity and drive to offer a strong attacking intent. The reality is that our defence is not as outstanding as some people seem to think it is, and what we have achieved at the back is often partly a result of a noticeably defensive midfield. The sooner we learn to judge our own abilities in a humble manner the quicker we can move forward; maybe a balance is now being reached between defence and attack.

Our first unchanged team of the season speaks volumes and after stabilising the ship we now face back-to-back home games at Fortress Mem against our loveable friends from the village of West Wycombe.

What could possibly go wrong?

# I dream of the JPT (part one)

### published on Thursday 22th October 2015

---

### *Saturday 3rd October - League Two*

## Morecambe  3    Bristol Rovers  4

Miller - 43', Archaize - 60',      Mansell - 28', Bodin - 47',
Mullin - 87' (pen)      Taylor - 58' , Harrison - 80' (pen)

**Rovers:** Nicholls [Booked], J Clarke, Lockyer, McChrystal, Brown,
Bodin (Leadbitter - 88'), Mansell, Sinclair, Gosling,
Easter (Harrison - 74'), Taylor (O Clarke - 82').

*Unused Substitutes:* Mildenhall, Montaño, Parkes, Lines.

Attendance: 1,712 inc 386 Gasheads

Referee: Andy Madley

---

### *Tuesday 6th October - Football League Trophy - Southern Round Two*

## Bristol Rovers  2    Wonky Wanderers  0

Taylor - 4', Easter - 11'

**Rovers:** Nicholls, Leadbitter, Parkes, McChrystal, Brown,
Bodin, Sinclair (O Clarke  - 74'), Lines, Montaño (Lyttle - 90+1'),
Easter (Blissett - 88'), Taylor.

*Unused Substitutes:* Mildenhall, Kilgour.

Attendance: 3,243 inc 123 Wonkers

Referee: Oliver Langford

---

### *Saturday 17th October - League Two*

## Mansfield Town  1    Bristol Rovers  2

Tafazolli - 81'      Easter - 15', Taylor - 90'+8

**Rovers:** Nicholls [Booked], Leadbitter (Harrison - 45' [Booked]), J Clarke, Lockyer,
Parkes, Brown,
Sinclair, Lines [Booked] (O Clarke - 45'), Mansell (Gosling - 84'),
Easter [Dismissed], Taylor.

*Unused Substitutes:* Mildenhall, Montaño, McChrystal, Blissett.

Attendance: 4,196 inc 847 Gasheads

Referee: Mark Haywood (2nd time this season)

**Tuesday 20th October - League Two**

## Bristol Rovers  0    Notts County  0

**Rovers:** Nicholls, Leadbitter, Lockyer, McChrystal, Brown, Bodin (Montaño - 72'), Mansell, Sinclair, Gosling, Harrison (Easter - 45'), Taylor (Blissett - 72').

*Unused Substitutes:* Mildenhall, Parkes, O Clarke, Lines.

Attendance: 6,743 inc 148 Magpies

Referee: Steve Martin

---

⊗  **In recent Rovers news**  ⊗

☠ The League match on 10th October against old friends Wonky Wanderers is postponed due to the internationals call-ups of Ellis Harrison, Tom Lockyer (both Wales Under-21's) and Jake Gosling (Gibraltar).

☠ Jermaine Easter's straight red at Field Mill for a phantom head butt after OTT aggravation from Nicky 'rhyming slang' Hunt was later rescinded by a panel of experts who were not registered blind. Hunt probably needs bed-time therapy because I'm not sure how he manages to sleep at night.

After receiving a First Round bye in the Johnstone's Paint Trophy (JPT), and smiting the mighty Chairboys in the Second Round we were rather suddenly propelled into the Area Quarter-Finals and just three fixtures from Wembley.

The JPT match was certainly value for money and a joy to watch, with both teams entering the field at breakneck speed. As much as I dislike the Chairboys for their disgraceful handling of the abandoned match in 2012, you have to admire the way they played in the first half, with pace, passing and positivity. It left them open at the back though and after a quick two goal blast Gasheads were in JPT dreamland.

Wycombe's best chance of a come back seemed to be a high tempo game, and the ref seemed determined to help them out, allowing every bad challenge to slip by him and the game to resemble an endless, but breathtaking, tennis rally. Somehow we managed to weather the storm (pun intended), aided by poor finishing and a couple of great saves from Lee Nicholls.

In the second half a normal game of error strewn League Two style football broke out, with aerial percentage football in the ascendancy and limbs noticeably tiring. Wycombe were now more akin to choirboys and Rovers, and Darrell Clarke, deserve credit for silencing them as the game changed.

One of the most remarkable moments of the match happened at kick-off, but didn't even get a mention. Whilst strikers and young starlets are endlessly debated in modern football the wonderful simplicity surrounding our longest serving player was summed up when Lee Brown's 200th appearance for the Gas wasn't even noticed.

Not only is the ever dependable, and never injured, Mr. Brown our only player to play every minute of our season so far, but this man is a true stalwart, and at barely 25 years old still has years ahead of him. A double century of games in itself is quite a feat considering his debut only came four years ago, on the 6th of August 2011, the televised season opener that marked AFC Wimbledon's first ever game in the Football League.

All hail our own soul sensation, the hardest working man in football, Lee James Brown.

We really need to win the JPT soon. Or do we really not need the distraction, the extra games, and potential extra injuries?

That was the question I asked fellow Gasheads on the Internet a few months ago, before the season got underway.

After analysing the Internet poll I started, whilst most of the 61 votes agreed it was good to win it, with only 3 votes wanting to forget it, the consensus was to treat it seriously but not at the expense of the League and to see it as more meaningful as we potentially get closer to Wembley.

My own slightly gung ho attitude is always that I want to win it. But why I asked myself?

**My first reason** is because our only proper Cup 'silverware' has been the Watney Cup in 1972-73. And let's be honest, no-one has heard of it, even though we beat top flight Wolverhampton Wanderers and Sheffield United to earn it. We've twice been Division Champions (1952/53 & 1989/90), where you get a cup, and had two play-off wins where you strangely also get a cup.

These pieces of silverware are particularly bizarre (the 2006/7 version of which came after only finishing sixth in the League) because we didn't get a cup in 1973/74 when finishing runners-up in a very competitive Third Division.

We're not going to win the F.A. Cup or the Football League Cup, so we might as well go for the JPT with all guns blazing.

**My second reason** for wanting to win it is because it feels like everyone else has won it apart from us. This isn't actually true but it seems like it, especially when Grimsby Town, Chesterfield, Wrexham, Mansfield Town and Rotherham United have all won it, but not us.

Can we console ourselves that Swindon Town, Burnley and Millwall have all lost their solitary appearance in the final? Not really. Or that several of the 'bigger' teams regularly seen in the two lower divisions, such as Bradford City, Notts County, Oxford United, Northampton Town, Oldham Athletic, Plymouth Argyle and Gillingham have never even reached a final?

Ok, maybe. I surprised myself when I researched this article and found that fans of these proud clubs have never even had the chance to go to Wembley or the Millennium Stadium for such a day trip, whilst fans of Bristol clubs have been there seven times between them.

**My third reason** for wanting to win it is simply because it is there. Surely all football fans want to win everything that is put in front of them?

# Intermission

This is the perfect time to take a comfort break (a.k.a. have a wazz), whilst a dolly bird with a tray full of ice-creams wafts fragrantly past you on her way down to the front of the auditorium.

If you are under 35 years of age, or have never visited a cinema out in the sticks, you probably have no idea what I'm on about. But then again at that age you may not get half the music and cultural references in this book either.

You know what, I might as well just pack up and go home now... put the pen and ink down, strap on my virtual reality goggles, eat some space food, and find something else to do instead.

Well, at this point of the season I kind of did just that.

I took a break from writing because it was a critical time of the year for me, and I was pulling together not just one, but two new books: 'Print That Season!', my story of our dramatic escape from the Conference; and, my unique 'Banksy Drawing & Colouring Book'.

Both are still available from me for less than a bag of magic beans.

So, before I get back to sharing my next article with you, I present for your delectation details of all the games whilst I was away, plus some of the key Pirate news up to December.

---

### *Saturday 24th October - League Two*

**Bristol Rovers  1     Newport County AFC  4**

Bodin - 15'      Parkes - 13' (og), Ansah - 52' & 57', O'Sullivan - 75'

**Rovers:** Nicholls, Leadbitter, Lockyer, Parkes, Brown, Gosling (Montaño - 67'), Sinclair, Mansell (Lines - 66'), Bodin, Easter (Harrison - 73'), Taylor.

*Unused Substitutes:* Mildenhall, O Clarke, J Clarke, Blissett.

Attendance: 7,442 inc 518 Exiles

Referee: Nick Kinseley

---

### *Friday 30th October - League Two*

## Cambridge United  1    Bristol Rovers  2

Corr - 33'      Harrison - 66', Taylor - 82'

**Rovers:** Nicholls, J Clarke [Booked], Lockyer, McChrystal, Brown, Gosling, Sinclair, Mansell, Bodin, Harrison, Easter (Taylor - 63').

*Unused Substitutes:* Mildenhall, Montaño, Leadbitter, Parkes, Lines, O Clarke.

Attendance: 5,115 inc 562 Gasheads

Referee: Brendan Malone (2nd time this season)

---

### *Sunday 8th November - F.A. Cup First Round*

## Bristol Rovers  0    Chesham United  1

Blake - 77'

**Rovers:** Nicholls, Leadbitter (J Clarke - 73'), Lockyer [Booked], McChrystal, Brown, Gosling, Sinclair, Mansell [Booked] (Lines - 62'), Bodin, Harrison, Taylor (Easter - 62').

*Unused Substitutes:* Mildenhall, Montaño, Parkes, Lucas.

Attendance: 5,181 inc 577 Generals (it seems like a funny way to run an army, but that honestly is their nickname)

Referee: Andy Davies (2nd cup game this season)

---

## ⊗  Statto Alert  ⊗

☠ After failing to score in four of our first six League games at the Mem Rovers scored in all of the next 17, starting from Newport County AFC.

☠ At the end of the season Rovers fans were rather shocked to discover that Lee Brown was the only defender to score all year.  Contrary Gasheads pointed out that Tom Parkes had scored an own goal though.

☠ Despite the fact that Chesham United, from three tiers (or 75 places) below us, played really well (and deserve huge credit for that), it was statistically the worst Rovers defeat in our history.  It was also the first time Rovers had lost at home in the FA Cup to non-league opposition and to rub salt into the wounds it was later voted the 'FA Cup Giant Killing of the Season'.

**Wednesday 11th November - Football League Trophy - Southern Qtr-Final**

## Southend United 1   Bristol Rovers 0

White - 11'

**Rovers:** Nicholls, J Clarke [Booked], McChrystal [Booked], Parkes, Brown,
Gosling (Montaño - 57'), Sinclair, Lines, Bodin,
Taylor, Easter (Lucas - 72').

*Unused Substitutes:* Mildenhall, O Clarke, Kilgour.

Attendance: 3,495 inc 181 Gasheads

Referee: Andy Woolmer

---

**Saturday 14th November - League Two**

## Bristol Rovers 2   Carlisle United 0

Taylor - 66' & 87'

**Rovers:** Nicholls, J Clarke, McChrystal [Booked], Parkes [Booked], Brown [Booked],
Montaño (Gosling - 83'), Lines (O Clarke - 90+2'), Sinclair [Booked], Bodin,
Taylor, Easter (Blissett - 89').

*Unused Substitutes:* Mildenhall, Mansell, Lucas, Kilgour.

Attendance: 6,423 inc 353 Cumbrians

Referee: Mark Brown

---

## ⊗ In recent Rovers news ⊗

⚜ Millwall forward Paris Cowan-Hall joins on a one month loan. That is probably the first time the place names 'Millwall' and 'Paris' have ever been used in the same sentence.

⚜ Billy Bodin's excellent performances are enough to deserve a contract extension to the end of the season.

⚜ Cambridge United forward Rory Gaffney joins on loan until January.

⚜ Nathan Blissett leaves again on the Conference loan bus, this time for perennial underachievers Lincoln City. Despite discovering he's only been bought a one-way ticket Nathan says there is no need to be upset.

### *Saturday 21st November - League Two*

## Crawley Town 2    Bristol Rovers 1
Murphy - 9' & 10'    Taylor - 87' (pen)

**Rovers:** Nicholls, J Clarke (Gosling - 76'), McChrystal (Lockyer - 45' [Booked]), Parkes, Brown [Booked], Montaño (Harrison - 45'), Lines, Sinclair, Bodin, Taylor, Easter.

*Unused Substitutes:* Mildenhall, Leadbitter, Mansell, O Clarke.

Attendance: 2,612 inc 836 Gasheads

Referee: Trevor Kettle (2nd time this season)

### *Saturday 28th November - League Two*

## Exeter City 1    Bristol Rovers 1
Reid - 90+4'    Sinclair - 83'

**Rovers:** Nicholls, Leadbitter (Bodin - 72'), J Clarke, Parkes, Lockyer, Brown, Sinclair, Mansell, O Clarke [Booked], Taylor [Booked] (Easter - 78'), Gaffney (Harrison - 78').

*Unused Substitutes:* Mildenhall, McChrystal, Lines, Cowan-Hall.

Attendance: 5,548 inc 1,559 Gasheads

Referee: Phil Gibbs

### *Tuesday 1st December - League Two*

## Bristol Rovers 3    Wonky Wanderers 0
Taylor - 60', 62' & 72'

**Rovers:** Nicholls, Leadbitter (Cowan-Hall - 79'), J Clarke, Lockyer, Parkes, Brown, Sinclair, Mansell, O Clarke (Bodin - 58'), Taylor (Easter - 84'), Gaffney.

*Unused Substitutes:* Mildenhall, McChrystal, Harrison, Montaño.

Attendance: 6,136 inc 255 Wonkers

Referee: Brendan Malone (3rd time this season)

# I dream of the JPT (part two)

### published on Friday 18th December 2015

*Saturday 12th December - League Two*

**Bristol Rovers 2    York City 1**

Easter - 71', Taylor - 90'+1    Oliver - 41'

**Rovers:** Nicholls, J Clarke (Leadbitter - 55'), Parkes, Lockyer, Brown, Cowan-Hall (Gosling - 55'), Mansell, Sinclair, Bodin (Easter - 70'), Taylor [Booked], Gaffney.

*Unused Substitutes:* Mildenhall, McChrystal, Harrison, O Clarke.

Attendance: 6,916 inc 170 Minstermen

Referee: Ben Toner

---

### ⊗   In recent Rovers news   ⊗

Matty Taylor is named PFA Fans' Player of the Month for November. With merely three goals in the month (one of which was his only penalty of the season), maybe his all-round play was finally being recognised?

Matty also scored a winner on 30th October and a hat-trick on 1st December, so maybe those subconsciously influenced the judges as well?

---

A while ago, before being knocked out by Southend United (again) I started my explanation as to why I wanted us to win the Johnstone's Paint Trophy (JPT) soon. Now the dust has settled on my new book, please let me recap the first three reasons and finish the rest.

**My first reason** was because our only proper Cup 'silverware' has been the Watney Cup in 1972-73. And let's be honest, no-one outside of a BS post-code remembers that ill-fated competition.

**My second reason** for wanting to win it was because it feels like everyone else has won it apart from us. This isn't actually true but it seems like it.

**My third reason** was simply because it is there. Surely all football fans want to win everything that is put in front of them?

**My fourth reason** for wanting to win it is because I feel deflated at getting so close on four previous occasions.

We've had two losses in the final of course, in 1990 to Tranmere Rovers, and 2007 against Doncaster Rovers, plus two losses in the Southern Area Final. Given our record against teams called Rovers thank God there was no chance of us playing a certain team from Blackburn this season! Our record in the competition is actually pretty good; 17th best out of the 71 clubs who have played more than 20 games in it.

But only two non-winners have lost it more times than us; Brentford and Southend United, losers for all three of their appearances. Carlisle United have gone astray in the final a calamitous four times, but at least they have won it twice for their far flung fans.

Our most agonising Southern Area Final loss was to Shrewsbury Town in March 1996 when we were a really good team and probably let our hugely successful run-in to the two-legged tie affect the final hurdle. To get that far we had already beaten teams that with present day glasses on looks like a who's who of clubs on the up - Brighton & Hove Albion, AFC Bournemouth, Fulham, Peterborough United, and Cambridge United.

The Auto Windscreen Shield, as it was known at that point, had adopted the Golden Goal rule for extra time and Marcus Stewart was the first Gashead to use it to win a game for us, at Craven Cottage in front of a pitiful crowd of less than 3,500 souls - which makes you wonder where all the fair weather Fulham fans crawled from during their 13 subsequent seasons in the Premier League?

A 1-1 draw at Gay Meadow came courtesy of someone called Damian Matthew, his only goal in a Rovers shirt during a 10 match loan spell from Crystal Palace, and people had an eye on the Final. But we unexpectedly lost 1-0 at Twerton in front of over 7,000 fans. In our home league match against the Shrews just ten days earlier Stewie scored a penalty to win the match, one of four successful penalties that campaign, but this time Mr.Cool curiously had his 56th minute penalty saved, and Ian Stevens scored for the Shrews 17 minutes later, his third goal in three games against us that season. It seemed like we had done the hard work, only to fall at the final hurdle.

Bristol Rovers; snatching defeat from the jaws of victory since 1883!

By 2004-05 the much maligned Ian Atkins had stopped the Rovers rot, making us the draw specialists in League Two. He also got us to the Southern

Area Final after four consecutive wins - proper wins, no Extra Time or pens, and I was one of less than 2,000 at a freezing Brisbane Road when none of us wanted the looming extra-time on a work day in January 2005, only to be sent unexpectedly wild by Lewis Haldane's last minute 'come from behind' winner in the Southern Semi-Final.

But the elation of that night in East London was undone when we lost 2-1 to Southend United in the home leg of the Southern Final, and a 2-2 draw at Roots Hall wasn't enough to rescue the aggregate, in a tie watched by in excess of 15,000 fans overall. Sending out a five-man midfield at the Mem didn't help, nor did a fluffed penalty from Junior Agogo, but at least this time we failed against a team generally considered to be better than us that season, as they gaining promotion out of the bottom division via a Play-Off win in Cardiff.

Shrimpers fans could have been forgiven for feeling nervous that day in Wales; they had already lost the Trophy final, to Wrexham, and after being top of League Two with just three games to go, had suddenly dropped three places into the play-offs! As their season threatened to fall apart they managed to hold their nerve, returning to the Millennium Stadium to beat Lincoln City after extra time.

**My fifth and final reason** is probably the best. Even though I'm not a superstitious person, I find it creepily bizarre that three times since I started following Rovers, Bristol football has been mutually successful for an entire season. Rovers and City were both promoted in 1990, 2007 and 2015, and in each of those seasons swathes of red or blue adorned the final of the Trophy; Rovers losing in 1990 and 2007, and City winning it in 2015 for a very impressive League One and Trophy double.

There were 17 seasons between the first and second times this 'annus gertluscious' occurred, yet only eight between the second and third happenings. That should mean it will only be four years for the next visitation of JPT's Comet, and the accompanying promotion.

Yes, you heard it here first people, Martin de Nostradamus Bull has predicted that City and Rovers will both get promoted in 2019, and one of them will get to the JPT final as well (hopefully City, as we plan to be in the Championship that season).

# champagne for the tinkerman?

### published on Thursday 31st December 2015

---

*Saturday 19th December - League Two*

## Dagenham & Redbridge  0    Bristol Rovers  3

Brown - 33', Gaffney - 83',
Bodin - 90'+5'

**Rovers:** Puddy (Mildenhall - 50'), Leadbitter (Bodin - 67'), J Clarke,  Lockyer,
Parkes [Booked], Brown,
Sinclair (Gosling - 50'), Mansell, O Clarke,
Taylor, Gaffney [Booked].

*Unused Substitutes:* McChrystal, Harrison, Cowan-Hall, Easter.

Attendance: 1,820 inc 603 Gasheads

Referee: Charles Breakspear

---

*Saturday 26th December - League Two*

## AFC Wimbledon  0    Bristol Rovers  0

**Rovers:** Mildenhall, J Clarke (Leadbitter - 45' [Booked]), Lockyer, McChrystal,
Brown,
Bodin, Mansell, O Clarke, Gosling (Montaño - 65'),
Taylor, Harrison (Gaffney - 73').

*Unused Substitutes:* Preston, Easter, Parkes, Broom.

Attendance: 4,668 inc 806 Gasheads

Referee: Keith Hill

---

### ⊗   In recent Rovers news   ⊗

Wimbledon was not quite a repeat of the infamous Woking Lockout (see
'Print That Season!' for details), but it was a minor shambles.  The Boxing
Day game at a small stadium was never made all ticket for either set of
supporters, but the Dons had to shut the doors to home fans by lunchtime,
and the away end didn't stay open much longer.

If 'Tea for the Tillerman' was Cat Stevens' breakthrough album exactly 45 years ago, what price on this season being Darrell Clarke's magnum opus?

This time of year gives a clear indication of how your season is shaping up, having played everyone once, although strangely in our case we have played six of the other top eight teams at home, and only one away, whereas it is the opposite against those teams currently placed 10th to 17th. Whilst there doesn't seem to be any real pattern to our results thus far, except excellent away results, the overall position is more than many expected.

Sixth place and enjoying the second best away record is certainly a remarkable achievement, even if a brace of clubs below us, and one just above us, have a game or three in hand on us. Being in a play-off place should not be taken for granted, especially when our only direct comparators (Barnet) languish in 18th and possess the worst away record in League Two. As we have seen many times this season margins are tight in football; just ask our noisy neighbours, who had a large bid accepted for an up and coming striker, only for him to decide to go elsewhere, and then score a haunting hat-trick against them. So you might as well enjoy the times you're on the right side of the knife edge.

In our nine previous seasons of bottom tier football ('the easiest League in England to escape' ™ ) Rovers were consistently no-where near the top half of the table by mid-season, and thus had little chance of a getting out of this division (the right way at least). In fact our average position on New Year's Eve was a dismal 17th. How can you have a successful season if you constantly run the first half of a marathon struggling along in a fancy dress clown outfit three sizes too big for you?

Darrell Clarke has three promotions in four seasons as a manager, which makes the negative attitude to his 'tinkering' even more galling. This negativity happened a lot last season, especially when not doing so well (no surprise there...), and it has certainly returned this season.

I can appreciate that five changes at AFC Wimbledon did seem a lot when seen briefly on a press report, but those changes didn't deserve the meltdown that happened in some minds. They say you should stick to writing what you know about so outside of Bristol Rovers my other topic is the artist Banksy, and he once wrote that, "A lot of people never use their initiative because no-one told them to." In football it seems that a lot of people never analyse the evidence because they can't be bothered to, or because it doesn't fit into their pre-conceived suppositions.

Injuries to Will Puddy, Stuart Sinclair and Daniel Leadbitter led to three of the changes, including a 'no brainer' start for Steve Mildenhall. Mark McChrystal was most probably favoured over Tom Parkes as his man marking perform- ances against big strikers have been impressive (just ask Jon Parkin, who spent two days living in his sweaty pocket during the play-off games six months ago), and strikers rarely come any bigger than Adebayo 'The Beast' Akinfenwa.

Ellis Harrison was most probably favoured over Rory Gaffney to provide a different problem to the Dons back-line, and to give Gaffney a slight rest and Harrison some much needed game time before the end of Gaffney's loan period and the busy holiday period. And whilst we may not all agree with Gosling and Bodin being the chosen pairing to start on the wings, surely we can understand the logic behind the change, especially when setting up in a 4-4-2 at Kingsmeadow, rather than the 3-5-2 used at Dagenham & Redbridge.

I feel we should consider ourselves fortunate to have players well coached in the ability to play different roles for different projects, rather than jumping to the conclusion that we have a manager who has a limited attention span and players who can't specialise.

In more general terms I can see four clear lines of reasoning in favour of taking a more prosaic approach to the inevitable 2pm team sheet release where between two and four changes will usually be announced.

Firstly, DC has always considered each game to be a different 'project'. I can't see how anyone can argue with that. Imagine if every piece of work you undertook, every sales call you made, every customer you served, every bathroom you tiled, or every child you taught, was rigidly given exactly the same resources, ticked off a dull checklist. You'd get mediocrity at best, and unmistakable failure when one size didn't fit all.

I am very glad that our manager looks at each game and tries to give us the best possible chance to win the match given the resources at his disposal that day. I wouldn't expect anything less from a professional manager. Often this approach will involve changes, although other times it may not.

Secondly, we are hardly blessed with many players who will be 'first on the team sheet' type picks, those who are rarely omitted or asked to play elsewhere for a different 'project'. Lee Brown is probably the only player at the club who has little competition for his place, and as an almost ever present for his four and a half seasons so far at Rovers, I personally don't feel this is a problem position anyway, as he does an admirable job, be it as a left back, or as a left wing-back. Currently Stuart Sinclair, Tom Lockyer and maybe Matty Taylor are the only other undroppables, and even they may be offered a 'rest' under my next point.

Thirdly, squad rotation is always a difficult issue for any manager, and any set of fans. If the tinkered with team plays well the manager is suddenly a genius, but if they lose he's pilloried like Claudio Ranieri was at Chelsea, even though he improved them every season and set the foundation for Mourinho's success. Keeping a squad of 20+ professional football players happy, especially competitive men when not regularly playing, must be one of the hardest aspects of being a manager, and it seems to me that DC is doing it pretty well. Maybe we should let him get on with it, especially when faced with two games in three days?

Finally, and probably most significantly, why should we expect a young manager with new ideas to stick to the conventional wisdom of rigidly keeping the same side for every game? Returning to the Banksy theme, it makes me think of the time the illusive artist wrote in reference to 'thinking outside the box', that you should actually "collapse the box, and take a ... sharp knife to it".

Why let even the box itself, um... box you in?

# home and away

## published on Wednesday 6th January 2016

### *Monday 28th December - League Two*

## Bristol Rovers 2    Leyton Orient 1

Gaffney - 31' & 53'    Simpson - 45'+1

**Rovers:** Mildenhall, Leadbitter [Booked], Lockyer, Parkes [Booked], Brown, Bodin (J Clarke - 74'), Mansell, Sinclair [Booked], Montaño (O Clarke - 81'), Easter (Taylor - 67'), Gaffney.

*Unused Substitutes:* Preston, McChrystal, Gosling, Harrison.

Attendance: 9,836 inc 487 Orienteers

Referee: Kevin Johnson (2nd time this season)

### *Saturday 2nd January - League Two*

## Bristol Rovers 2    Luton Town 0

Gaffney - 60' & 72'

**Rovers:** Mildenhall, Leadbitter, J Clarke, Lockyer, Parkes, Brown, Sinclair, Mansell, O Clarke, Taylor [Booked] (Easter - 87'), Gaffney (Harrison - 90'),

*Unused Substitutes:* Preston, Lines, McChrystal, Bodin, Montaño.

Attendance: 9,131 inc 707 Mad Hatters

Referee: Lee Swabey

### ⊗   In recent Rovers news   ⊗

☠ Rory Gaffney made rather TOO much of an impact though, leading to cries of 'sign him up' and a short-lived Mexican stand-off as Cambridge United realised they suddenly had a bit more power over his possible transfer than before his four exemplary goals in two games.

☠ Young right back Tyler Lyttle goes on loan to the end of the season with Nuneaton Town, our old acquaintances from the Conference season.

No, this isn't a blog about a tired old Aussie soap, but a look at how important away results can be. It seems like no coincidence that our swift rise up the table has come at a time when we've suddenly won five out of six home games, AND crucially continued to keep the away points rapidly ticking over.

Whilst conventional wisdom says that you cannot rely on away form, our incredible record has now lasted so long that it might now be the time to kick that old chestnut into the stingers and let it rot alongside the discarded crisp packets and abandoned jazz mags.

We are not alone though. Although our away record is uniquely in the 'truly exceptional' category (only a brace of away day blanks since mid September 2014; a staggering record of won 16, drawn 14, lost 2), there seems to be a growing trend of away prowess in our current League. 13 teams have a better away record than home, and only two of the 11 on the opposite side of the fence (Barnet and Notts County) could be considered to possess the time-honoured combination of a home record that is substantially better than their disappointing away results.

Our own league track record on the road this season is a outstanding Won 7, Drawn 3 and Lost 2. Only Plymouth Argyle have a better record. The caveat we may need to add though is that we have only played one of the current top seven teams away, although the caveat on top of the caveat (if that is feasible) is that although in a lower position now, Leyton Orient were actually top of the table when we faced them and Mansfield Town were fourth.

Points on the road can be incredibly important to a season. We were languishing in 17th spot after losing to Portsmouth in late September, one of four losses in five games, but a trio of away wins followed and our season was suddenly resurrected. Indeed, several fans, and our manager himself, have said that that rather surprising 3-0 trouncing of Hartlepool United on a Tuesday night (our longest trip of the season - thanks fixture computer, I hope your CPU dies tomorrow) was our best result of the season so far.

I realise I've used the following stat before, but it is so darn remarkable it deserves repeating, if only to serve as a warning to teams who neglect their away performances. Gillingham got relegated from League One in the 2009/10 season despite earning 44 points at the Priestfield Stadium. A derisory six away points saw them go down on goal difference.

If continued away defeats are cataclysmic, a sudden loss of away form is also debilitating, so we must be on our guard, especially with a very difficult run of away games coming up (Barnet, Oxford Utd, Accrington Stanley, Portsmouth and Wycombe). Bury are currently on a seven match losing run on the road in League One, and despite three home wins out of four during this period, have dropped from fourth to 14th. Is this the most fascinating statistic of Bury's recent history? Not really, as before the calamitous losing streak they were our main rival for a startling away record, not having tasted defeat since January, a sequence of 15 games unbeaten (won 12, drawn 3).

But feast or famine is rarely a way to foster longer term success.

Next up on our travels are our old friends Barnet. The Bees have the third best home record in League Two, but the worst away record, which should make for a fascinating clash. The chink of light in their armour is that they've only taken four home points against the five teams they have so far faced from the top half of the table. This is no complete surprise, and is merely an exaggeration of their performances last season, being superlative flat track bullies against the lower teams, and also rarely obtaining the mediocrity of a draw.

That brings me onto another truism, that regularly drawing is not much good in modern football. Witness Leyton Orient's recent fall from 6th to 10th whilst on a seemingly impressive four match unbeaten run. The problem was that they were all 1-1 draws.

Whilst we were the away draw specialists last season, with a dozen of them giving us our highest seasonal tally in our history, we have certainly changed this season, as since back in the Football League draws have only made up 25% of our away results.

Home and away, I just hope we can keep any loss of form at bay until the summer.

# if you can't stand the heat, get out of the kitchen

### published on Tuesday 19th January 2016

---

*Saturday 9th January - League Two*

## Barnet 1    Bristol Rovers 0

Hoyte - 5'

**Rovers:**  Mildenhall, Leadbitter, J Clarke (Easter - 64'), Lockyer [Booked],
Parkes, Brown,
Sinclair, Mansell (Lawrence - 65'), O Clarke (Lines - 45'),
Taylor, Harrison.

*Unused Substitutes:* Preston, McChrystal, Bodin, Montaño.

Attendance: 2,770 inc 1,262 Gasheads

Referee: Michael Bull [I have a cousin who shares that name, but sadly it wasn't him]

---

### ⊗    In recent Rovers news    ⊗

☠ 5th January marked the end of an era as Nathan Blissett left Rovers by mutual consent.  As Nathan waved goodbye he left Gasheads a parting pearl of wisdom - 'there is no need to be upset'.  And like a puff of smoke the enlightened one was gone, spirited away to a better place.  Or Torquay.

☠ Midfielder Liam Lawrence joined Rovers until the end of the season after cash strapped League One strugglers Shrewsbury Town let him leave by the old 'mutual consent'. Unfortunately his final memory was playing 60 painful minutes of their 7-1 mauling at the hands of Chesterfield.

---

The title of this piece was regularly used by the American President Harry S Truman, a plain speaker who wouldn't pass the spin doctor filter these days, and who must have known a thing or two about heat, being the President who ordered the two nuclear attacks on Japan in 1945.

The true test of a person's character is when things aren't going well, or to use a biblical analogy anyone can love those loving you; what is far harder is loving those who oppose you, or even shout things at you.

In a week when another in a long line of local managers proved he just couldn't handle it when things go badly (Paul Buckle, Sean O'Driscoll and numerous other suspect leaders of both Bristol sides also spring to mind) we can reflect on another attribute to admire in Darrell Clarke.

Although he's a slightly prickly and aloof character at times, he has proven to be pretty good at handling the few mini-crises he has faced in almost six seasons in management. Admittedly we've never seen him in a 'normal' full-blown crisis, and although the eight games he was given to save us in 2014 were obviously unsuccessful, it is hard to judge him on that as there were so many complicating factors in those five weeks, including those numbers themselves, eight and five; simply not hefty enough.

The two mini-crises us Gasheads have seen at first hand have been during the balmy first blooms of each season. If some Gasheads were champing at the bit in early September 2014, after away defeats at Barnet, Altrincham and Braintree Town, September 2015 was treated with slightly less kerfuffle even though after seven games we had only one point more than 2014's seemingly apocalyptic start, had scored a miserly five goals (the joint fewest in the division), and most importantly were on an unwanted three game losing streak, with a triple barrelled blank up front. A further loss and a draw left us 17th and rather ruffled.

Yet both times DC turned the ship around, grinding out five victories on the trot in a packed 19 day period in September 2014, and a year later embarking on three fine away wins in a row, scoring nine goals in the process; two more than in the entire nine previous League games. At our nadirs Darrell's team were 19th and 17th, yet he didn't buckle and hauled us up to second and fifth (so far).

At Salisbury City Darrell never allowed any real troughs, but there were relative lows, all of which were tackled with the grit and professionalism he is now well known for.

For the 2010/11 season DC and Mikey Harris were thrown in the deep end after financial problems and an enforced double relegation. With the club in chaos they managed to remain undefeated in the opening seven Southern Premier games, but draws were costing them badly, and as the likes of Cambridge City, Truro City and our friends Chesham United had started with louder bangs, they found themselves only fourth, with a thumping 3-0 loss then tipping them into fifth.  Now, fifth may not sound like a crisis to many, but for a 'big' club in the seventh tier of football, where only the champions get automatic promotion, it was a mini-pickle; a pile of discarded fast food burger gherkins perhaps?

The Whites responded with a 17 game unbeaten run (13 of them wins), and finally hit top spot in February.  A 6-0 home massacre at the hands of Truro City seemed like a blip, but a poor run-in of only eight points from the final eight games dumped them into third spot.  Unperturbed, DC capably guided them through the play-offs, against teams in better form than them, both of whom had already beaten them during the regular season.

The 2011/12 season in Conference South was a stormy affair, yo-yoing around mid-table most of the season, and at one point negotiating a five match losing streak.  Success only came in the cups, with the Cathedral city reaching its first ever FA Cup Third Round.

2012/13 witnessed a different manner of pressure, as they topped the table for over four months, only to drop into second during a run of two draws and two defeats, and never made it back to the summit despite 20 points from their final nine games.  Darrell's charges dusted themselves down, kept their nerve and won the play-offs AGAIN.

One word seems to sum up the ultimate breakdown of our recent local failures; stubborn.

John Ward's stubborn resistance to pace and width, Mark McGhee's stubborn refusal to use players in their best positions nor join the modern era (like... er, the 20th Century), Sean O'Driscoll's stubborn rejection of football that might actually win games, and Steve Cotterill's stubbornness to change a formation and stop blaming everything except himself.

Thankfully DC is more often accused of the opposite; tinkering, trying new things, and keeping a relatively open mind.

The Rovers kitchen sometimes has the gas turned up too high, but don't be upset, Darrell Worrall-Clarke is in there cooking up a slice of level headed pie.

# let's dance
### published on Thursday 21st January 2016

---

*Sunday 17th January - League Two*

### Oxford United  1    Bristol Rovers  2
Roofe - 46'    Taylor - 52', Harrison - 88' (pen)

**Rovers:** Mildenhall, Leadbitter, J Clarke, Lockyer [Booked], Parkes, Brown, Sinclair, Mansell (O Clarke - 68'), Lines, Taylor (Easter - 76'), Gaffney (Harrison - 85').

*Unused Substitutes:* Preston, McChrystal, Bodin, Montaño.

Attendance: 9,492 inc 2,359 Gasheads

Referee: Nick Kinseley (2nd time this season)

---

### ⊗  In recent Rovers news  ⊗

☠ After a week of horse trading Rory Gaffney joins Rovers on a permanent contract for an undisclosed fee (believed to be around 32 horses, a dozen mules, and a zebra).

☠ Tom Lockyer was the recipient of The Football League Young Player of the Month for December award. Gasheads try to hush-up the attention received. Move along now, there's nothing to see here...

☠ Minutes after scoring the winner at Oxford United, DC has to explain to the press why Ellis Harrison is off on a months loan to Ice Station Zebra, a.k.a. Hartlepool United, under the rule of the brutish despot Prof. Ronald Moore. That will surely make him appreciate just how splendid Bristol is.

---

One thing we've certainly learnt from the past two seasons, and even a glimpse into Darrell Clarke's past at Salisbury City, is that his teams rarely come out of the blocks in August at full speed, but they certainly do pick up during the season. DC undoubtedly likes to build his teams slowly and do his business on a continual basis, rather than just during the traditional transfer window flurry. He rightly also prefers to get his limited signings in a window in early, as witnessed recently by snaffling Liam Lawrence from cash strapped Shrewsbury Town, and the rapid return of Rory Gaffney.

We now seem to be up into third or fourth gear and if last season was anything to go by, the final 19 League games could prove very interesting indeed. Rovers are into a period where six of our seven games are against teams in the top eight, and this should now be seen as an opportunity rather than a drag. Whatever the result of this difficult spell though we will always have plenty to fight for this season and with six of our final seven games against teams currently in the bottom 11 I hope the dancing shoes will be able to come out of the closet.

A thrilling win at Oxford United is hardly the stuff of legend (a QI stat shows that in our last seven encounters with the U's, the home team has never won) but given the hype surrounding Oxford at the moment and their excellent form, make no bones that this win will suddenly put us on the radar of others; not only teams around us in League Two, but also scouts and analysts wanting to find out how we've gone from 19th in non-league to fourth in League Two within 16 months, and maybe realising just how many good characters we have in our squad and how many young players with over 100 appearances are already catching the eye.

In a month when David Bowie alas departed this planet I was reminded of a childhood conundrum from the Nile Rodgers produced album that resurrected his career, 'Let's Dance'. As I lay in bed in 1983 I wondered just how moonlight could actually be serious. Three decades later and whilst I may still be none the wiser, I do now know that gas can finally be taken seriously.

Would Cambridge United really have loaned us Rory Gaffney if they knew that we'd go unbeaten for his seven games with us and stay above them, despite their own six match unbeaten run? Whilst I'm not suggesting they arrogantly didn't see us as a rival for a play-off spot, it was possibly a strange deal to allow considering our league positions, and seems to add fuel to the fire that Shaun Derry had little time for the ginger ninja and had a longer term loan or move in the back of his mind from the off. Watching Derry backtrack after Gaffers did so well here was like watching a clapped out oil tanker attempting a wheezing U-turn in midstream.

In comparison loaning a useful, but needy, striker like Ellis Harrison out to Hartlepool United seems a far less controversial choice of club; a play-off place for 'Pools is about as likely as mistaking a monkey for a French spy... isn't it?

I can't think of too many benefits that arise from being taken seriously now, and fans may have preferred us to remain under the radar longer, but a late storm up the table is just too risky. In May 2007 we were just four minutes away from missing out on the play-off spot that opened the door to an unlikely escape from a League where we were 16th in mid-March.

Sadly I can't let last week pass without a minor off the field comment. Not only was it three years since my gorgeous son was born, but 16th of January 2013 was also the day Bristol City Council resolved to grant Sainsbury's planning permission to build on the Mem. A day later the Section 106 agreement for the UWE Stadium was signed between Rovers, South Gloucestershire Council, Bristol City Council and the UWE itself. The official planning permission had also been granted earlier in that week on the 11th January.

Three years down the line the only silver lining in this disarray seems to be that the UWE planning permission lasts for five years. Little happens quickly with stadium projects so the two years we have left to lay down some bricks may come in handy.

On the field success has given rise to intense happiness over the past 16 months, but it is so sad to see that all the positivity and 'bums on seats' (or in our case feet on terraces) may still end up being frustrated by a relatively small short fall in funds. I have only been going to away games for 26 years, but even in my time I have seen massive changes in club stadia, yet very little in our own, from my nascent days on the Popular side at Twerton to current times on the Blackthorn / Bass / North Terrace at the Mem.

Elm Park, the Vetch Field, the Goldstone Ground, Leeds Road, Springfield Road, and many more were frankly decaying dog pits, yet where are those failing clubs now with their new fangle dangle stadiums? Many others may not have experienced sparkling success at their new homes but at least do have a tidy stadium with better facilities for players, fans, and business users alike, and don't have a Gay Meadow, a Layer Road, or a Saltergate hanging over them like a Victorian poorhouse. Others have redeveloped their grounds so they look almost like new builds.

Some oxygen thieves may take the mick out of Oxford United's three sided stadium, still stuck with the ownership and name of a previous egotistical Chairman and the mischievously entitled 'Fence End', but anyone who re-members the quaint but decrepit Manor Ground with its Meccano motif of about seven different higgledy-piggledy sections will put their laughter away and congratulate them for what they DO have, rather than focus on what they don't quite yet have.

# priced out

### published on Thursday 28th January 2016

---

*Saturday 23rd January - League Two*

### Bristol Rovers 1    Plymouth Argyle 1

Bodin - 79'    Simpson - 88'

**Rovers:** Mildenhall, Leadbitter, J Clarke (Bodin - 54'), Lockyer,
Parkes [Booked], Brown,
Sinclair, Mansell (Montaño - 54'), Lines,
Taylor (Easter - 73'), Gaffney.

*Unused Substitutes:* Preston, McChrystal, O Clarke, Broom.

Attendance: 10,190 inc 1,285 Janners

Referee: Oliver Langford

---

### ⊗   In recent Rovers news   ⊗

Ellis Harrison went straight into the Pools team for a Tuesday night encounter at Accrington Stanley. They lose 3-1. Manager Ronnie Moore utilises his incredible motivational powers to chastise his new frontline. Moore was sacked in February after seven points from his final 12 games.

Thankfully we have a young progressive manager today; I truly believe that most older managers are now dyed-in-the-wool dinosaurs.

---

Given our rise up the table and the positivity now surrounding the on-field performance of the club, this article is certainly a gamble of the likes not seen since £250,000 was thrown away on Mickey 'Plymouth Argyle Legend' Evans in August 2000, a transfer window panic buy after Jamie Cureton had got the move he so manoeuvred, cough, I mean politely requested. Eight months later he quietly slipped out the side exit for £30,000, like a thief in the night, and a dozen games afterwards we were relegated.

I wrote a good chunk of this article earlier in the season, but I left it to mellow and mature with age like a wheel of the finest Cheddar.

Having returned to it I can say, hand on heart, that I still believe the sentiment behind it is right. The economics may have changed but the facts have not. Gasheads may be happier at the moment, and may be more willing to go the extra mile to find the money to attend games, but the underlying issue has not been solved.

Watching Rovers at the Mem without a season ticket has been simply too expensive this season.

There has not been even ONE special ticket offer for League games so far this season; in fact it has been quite the opposite. Our loyalty when sticking with the club last season was rewarded with six expensive 'Category A' matches and the student discount being silently dumped without an explanation. This will easily be the least home games I have been able to afford since returning from geographical exile in 2010.

Even our shocking home form (a solitary League win from the first seven matches; and merely four points in total) wasn't enough to encourage the club to offer the plebs a deal. Despite regular defeats, a Tuesday match, and a Sunday lunchtime match live on Sky, the Board did not offer anything, not even a 'Quid a Kid' day. Would it be uncharitable to suggest that most of the regular attendees of around 6,500 home fans up to Christmas were Season Ticket holders, who were 'stuck' with their decision, and who are apparently counted, even if not even in the ground?

Ordinary people are being priced out of football, and don't kid yourself that it is only happening at the Arsenal's and Chelsea's of this world. It also happens in the lower leagues. In fact, on the occasions that I attend Championship or Premier League games with my Norwich City supporting best friend, watching that level of football, in modern stadiums with excellent sight lines, is rarely much more expensive than watching Rovers at the run-down Mem, and the quality of the game and the facilities is of a vastly higher level. Last season I parted with £23 to be alongside him at Wolves for their opening game of the season, and a few weeks ago a frankly outlandish £15 was all that was required to get into the away end at the Britannia Stadium for their Premier League clash.

Asking an adult to pay a 'Category A' £20 to stand at the Mem on either an end terrace with a terrible view (but a roof and a great atmosphere), or an open terrace with an ok view and less atmosphere, is rubbish. No game at League Two level should be a special category, unless it is a downwards category for a freezing cold evening in January as the credit card statement hits the post Christmas mat. If there ever happens to be a genuine local derby at this execrable level then surely the extra ticket sales and other money spinning add-ons associated with a more popular match should cover any extra Police bill or whatever lame excuse the football club come up with this time? It's not as though we don't usually have extra capacity to fill.

And what kind of twisted logic puts UP prices when a venue isn't even being filled, or tells its loyal supporters they must pay for extra costs associated with a larger crowd, and / or a larger away following - who incidentally aren't getting in for free but who will be adding tens of thousands of pounds into the club pot.

Premier League bosses defend some of their prices by pointing to a 96% occupancy rate, and with a shrug of the shoulders calculate they must be doing something right. So what humbling logic could we use, especially earlier in the season? That we had a 60% occupancy rate, so the most obvious decision will be to make it less affordable for more people to come?

I suppose this line of reasoning is halfway out the window now though, as we are finally doing well again at home, have had a trio of matches against well supported opposition, and a lot of the casuals have presumably come back since Christmas. The last three home games would be labelled 'cash cows' by economists; maximum profit for minimal effort. But sadly these games won't help the underlying problem; in fact you could argue they make it worse by providing easy pickings and a distraction from the improvements that need to be made. On the pitch success, fair ticket prices, and decent facilities seem to be the three ways to increase crowds in the long run, and only the first is definitely happening.

With 9,836 for Leyton Orient, 9,131 for the Hatters, and 10,190 when the Pilgrims contributed an away sell-out, the occupancy rate is now more like 80% and with only nine home games left (all distinctly winnable) the chance of pressurising the club to run some offers is presumably too late; the stable door is off its hinges by now and the filly is already six furlongs away.

A mind bending six League games this season have been included in the laughable Category A. That's 26% of home games. I have to pinch myself to remember that this is the Fourth Tier, which includes NO clubs we have serious beef with and no clubs with a really serious hooligan problem.

There is no Bristol City, no Swindon Town, and no Cardiff City. Instead we have Yeovil Town and Exeter City installed as phoney Category A matches, as if to try to invent some sort of intense rivalry. One is a non-descript local town who we've only played 15 times since 1883 (we've played Liverpool more times), and the other is a middle-class University city 100 miles away with anaemic crowds (an average of 3,783 last season). Neither fixture has any more taste or spice to it than the mildest Cauliflower Korma.

Whilst the flexi-ticket may be a decent enough idea, the bureaucracy surrounding it can be off putting, especially for exiles, and the price is hardly compelling as it works out at £14 a match, plus a £4 surcharge if you dare try to use them for those titanic Category A classico's.

For a huge city like Bristol, with well over 50,000 students, terminating the student category this season was a frankly pitiable decision. There is admittedly a new 16-21 category, but not only are the prices nowhere near as affordable as the previous student prices (£4 off most tickets, compared to £7 previously), but also not all students are under 21. Indeed in the modern era, more and more students are NOT under 21, and are proud of it, having taken years out, returned as 'mature students', or are doing post-graduate degrees, which is in itself is a massively booming market that Rovers seem to be ignoring precisely at the time they are trying to build the UWE Stadium on UWE land. You could hardly make it up.

If any readers defend all this by contending that some other clubs are worse that us, they have surely missed the point. Our benchmark should not be clubs who are worse than us, but should be clubs who are better than us. And comparing merely on price also isn't completely fair, as some other clubs do not have terracing, and may offer better facilities than ours.

I realise I'll take some flak for what may be dismissed by some as negativity within a positive few months, but a few wins does not make everything hunky dory.

Ordinary, average fans are being priced out of watching the team they support and whilst a season in non-league may have humbled the players and the fans, it doesn't seem to have done a lot for the number crunchers intent on squeezing as much money out of us as possible.

# the edge of heaven
### published on Wednesday 3rd February 2016

*Saturday 30th January - League Two*

## Accrington Stanley 1    Bristol Rovers 0
McConville - 69'

**Rovers:** Mildenhall, J Clarke, Lockyer, Parkes, Brown, Lawrence (Montaño - 76'), Sinclair, Mansell, Bodin (Easter - 76'), Taylor, Gaffney (Fallon - 76').

*Unused Substitutes:* Preston, McChrystal, Leadbitter, Lines.

Attendance: 2,027 inc 543 Gasheads

Referee: Mark Haywood (3rd time this season)

## ⊗  In recent Rovers news  ⊗

Rovers smash EU rules on Rory quotas by signing experienced New Zealander Rory Fallon on non-contract terms. I suspect he was the first NZ international at Rovers since Paul 'Release the Beast' Nixon graced Gerry Francis' late 80's team. Rory has an ice cream business as a sideline, which must have salivated the taste buds of players at Cribbs when they heard 'Greensleeves' being mashed through a tinny speaker.

Back in September I wrote an article for this blog entitled 'For every action there is an equal and opposite reaction'. We had just lost, as usual, to Accrington Stanley, and with seven games down we had only one point more than last seasons' seemingly apocalyptic start, had scored a miserly five goals (the joint fewest in the division), were on a three game losing streak and crowds were falling. The article postulated that Darrell Clarke would most probably respond well to this mini crisis.

A draw at Plymouth Argyle raised hopes but an anaemic home loss to Pompey dumped us into 17th place. The knives were being sharpened and knitted brows were the order of the day. Three away wins on the bounce though bought DC a lot of space from the careless whispers, and despite blips along the way we've generally been on a fantastic upwards trajectory to make it big ever since... until playing the reverse fixture at the newly re-named Wham Stadium of course; the first double any team has ever done over a Darrell Clarke led Rovers side.

It seems like the self styled "club that wouldn't die" just won't let us have any divine peace. Accy have won our last six encounters (including three succes-sive 1-0 wins in Horfield), during which we've scored just a solitary goal.

Curiously that goal from loanee Alex Henshall, in his sole start for us, came early in the game that was the start of the end of our 94 year unbroken tenure in the Football League. Although we were already struggling by mid-October 2013 most fans didn't expect a relegation battle, especially when one-up at rookie James Beattie's winless, bottom of the table Accring-ton Stanley. Two goals later and our expectations REALLY were being lowered.

Reports suggest that we never really got out of bed on Saturday, and for our next game we will need to wake up before we go. Our young guns never seemed to go for it, Stanley's midfield were given the freedom of the park, and wiser old heads were reported to be rather sluggish as though they were still working off last Christmas's excesses.

One thing I have learnt following football is that whatever managers articu-late about the dangers of away travel, the much sought after edge of heaven, where harmony, camaraderie and an overnight stay prevail, will still not guarantee a win on the road. Maybe it can help, but there are also days like Saturday when the lengths clubs go to get their players into the best possible mind and body shape seems to bear no fruit at all, unless it is a prickly pear perhaps.

When Rovers posted pictures on twitter of how good the pitch looked at 11am I thought to myself 'wow, they got up there fast'. I should have put two and two together rather quicker and realised they had spent the night in a Lancashire hotel.

The club had also posted a brilliant initiation 'song' from one of the new boys and whilst the venue hardly looked like an exotic Club Tropicana it was clearly filmed in something other than a bad boys dressing room. Rory Fallon had apparently been training with Rovers for a month and his hard work must have been screaming 'I'm your man' at DC. Rory's Maori mum had taught him well, as he bypassed a song and performed a haka, and with a hairy chest like that no-one was going to offer him outside on a cold Blackburn night.

Another explanation of the insipid defeat could be that however well you prepare Stanley are simply a better team than us at the moment. The heady days of our first encounter with them (a 4-0 trashing in December 2006) have long since gone, and since an equally overwhelming 5-1 butchery at the Mem in April 2012 it's been all downhill against them.

If in a cut throat top seven you truly are only as good as your last match then we really need a result against another phoenix club, AFC Wimbledon, this weekend. The Dons recently sneaked (temporarily) into the final play-off position and a plethora of teams hover around the 40+ points mark just waiting for any of the current play-off spot incumbents to have a mini-slump.

They also have an impressive away record, having lost only twice out of 14 away games, the last of which came way back in early October at high flying Oxford United.

Rovers have only suffered back-to-back league defeats three times in the last two seasons and I'll stick my neck out to predict that once DC gets them onto the training ground this week, we won't be seeing another such unwanted statistic this weekend.

---

If you hadn't already noticed this article included a secret word search inspired by the visit to the Wham Stadium, the slightly bizarre new name for Accrington Stanley's 'Crown Ground'.

There are 11 single or album titles from the nefarious 80's pop duo Wham! badly hidden in the piece:

2nd paragraph - 'Careless Whisper', 'Fantastic', and, 'Make it Big';

5th para - 'Wake Me Up Before You Go-Go' (almost got it in!), 'Young Guns (Go for It!), 'Freedom', and, 'Last Christmas';

6th para - 'The Edge of Heaven';

8th para - 'Club Tropicana', 'Bad Boys', and, 'I'm Your Man'.

# I don't want to go to Chelsea

### Published on Thursday 11th February 2016

> ⊗  **In recent Rovers news**  ⊗
>
> ☠ 543 hardy Gasheads braved the atrocious rain at Accrington Stanley and although we lost, as usual, Rovers had the last laugh on 7th May. Stanley held an impressive record of scoring in every home game of their season... until that final weekend blank against Stevenage.
>
> ☠ The scheduled home game against AFC Wimbledon was postponed due to a waterlogged pitch, our only game lost to the weather.

Whilst Elvis Costello's titular ditto may not be something you would often hear in 21st century football parlance, recent events leave me pondering whether a remix entitled 'I don't want to go to Bristol' could be genuinely applicable or is just an excuse for repeated local failure?

Many Rovers fans may be tempted to snigger behind the bike sheds at how difficult it has been for our noisy neighbours to sign any real life football players this season, but if we have any ambition ourselves we need to be careful to learn from their mistakes and mull over whether some of the headline grabbing excuses can affect us as well.

It is well documented that large bids for Andre Gray and Dwight Gayle were accepted by their own clubs, but neither decided to move to City; indeed Gayle never even came to check the vibe out.  Other summer targets also failed to get a one-way ticket to Temple Meads, and before they knew it City were left with a small squad, short on Championship experience and very short on league points.

They did have an expensive Director of Football though, and as we Gasheads well know, the second a DoF starts to either sign expensive flops, or not be able to sign anyone at all, is the second the head coach suddenly becomes the Eric Cantona genius of the relationship, and the DoF becomes the Didier Deschamps water carrier.  More recently bids for relatively unknown League One players such as Bradley Dack and Alex Gilbey never even got accepted by their clubs, and Zach Clough came, saw and did not cash the cheque.

What Robins must find particularly galling is that they not only have a billionaire as a benevolent owner, but also that they have a top heavy structure that really should have been able to get players in, with a Director of Football, and now also a Chief Operating Officer. If that structure cannot identify and land players you do wonder why on earth it exists.

We have rarely used a DoF position and when we did it was probably the right person at the right time, when Lennie Lawrence came in to team up with Paul Trollope, who was a rookie 33 year old coach at the time. Thankfully the next use of it was jettisoned pretty quickly, with John Ward barely half way up the flight of stairs before he was sacked following relegation.

Getting a good start to a season is of course amongst the opening chapters of the Dunce's Guide to Football, but watching City's problems spiral out of control should have really rammed it home to us how difficult life gets once you are struggling.

The lower you are the more the pressure gets to everyone involved and the less chance there is of the right players coming to join your relegation battle. A weak start and no clear and sustained improvement leaves a manager almost guaranteed to be walking a tightrope at exactly the time (i.e. the winter transfer window) when he needs to have his full wits about him, and the full backing of his Board, the players, and the fans.

We are certainly not immune to that feeling, and several times in recent seasons we have scuffed around in February and March trying to find decent loans and free agents. Invariably even the best manager will end up with the likes of Jerel Ifil. Enough said.

The main lesson we need to learn seems to be a simple one. Get your core business done in the summer and get it done as early as possible.

Thankfully this is something Darrell Clarke has proved to be pretty good at, although he also likes to continue to build squads slowly throughout the season, using his reputation as a 'tinker man' not only on match day but also on the overall squad.

Another lesson could be to get your marquee signing in first, and potentially even pay slightly over the odds if necessary to use him as bait for future targets and as an example of your serious intent. For the Robins the writing was on the wall by 10th August when owner Steve Lansdown was quoted as saying "It [the cost of Championship players] demonstrates the silliness of football. It's not a proper business".

As a very clever man who has become a billionaire without producing a single tangible product he may need to go back and look at the reality of what modern life is these days, and precisely how he earned his own wealth.

Which brings me onto the second part of this soliloquy. Is modern day Bristol really such an un-inviting place on a personal and geographical level? Do players really not want to go to Bristol?

Obviously I'm biased as a West Country lad, but I simply don't buy this excuse. Yes there are always human dynamics involved in any possible football transfer (are you close to friends and family where you currently are? do you really enjoy where you are in London, Oxford or even Wolverhampton? do you have kids settled at a school?) but to suggest the Bristol area may be putting players off beyond the above complications is surely bunkum.

Bristol is one of the most culturally dynamic cities in the whole of the UK, and is less than two hours from London on a train, has a decent airport, and has two of the countries' principal motorways running alongside it north and south, east and west.

Maybe players just don't know how agreeable our area is until they try it? Last week on Geoff Twentyman's new weekly BBC Radio Bristol 'Having a Gas' programme, Geoff not only had ex-Rovers man mountain Steve Elliott as a guest, a Derbyshire lad who came to Bristol in 2004 and still loves it here, but also regaled us with a personal tale of when he himself came down from Lancashire to sign for Rovers in 1986 and was told by local hero Harold Jarman that "you'll never move away", as he rattled off about five big names who came to the city and stayed. 30 years later and Harold's prediction is still accurate for Geoff.

I have however heard some lower league players declare that the high cost of living in many parts of the South does affect their quality of life, especially those with families. Championship wages may not make this an issue, but League Two wages can.

Is Bristol a footballing backwater?

Well, we have to hold our hands up on this one.

It just about typifies the laid back Bristolian mentality that it took Rovers almost 40 years of its early life before it joined the Football League and since then has enjoyed only 19 seasons in the Second Tier in nearly a century. City of course were in the League like a rat up a drainpipe, barely seven years after forming, but even they've only had nine seasons in the top division, and 53 in the Second Tier.

So when a player is weighing up his future and wondering which potential suitor might take him higher, a club like Burnley, with a relatively decrepit stadium and an icy Pennine breeze even in mid-July, can still tempt Andre Gray more than Bristol can.

That cycle is really hard to break and will affect even us, down in League Two, especially with spartan training facilities and a stadium made for rugby and virtually untouched for two decades.

There is little to snigger about here, only lessons to be learned and realities to be overcome.

# the future's so bright, i gotta wear shades
### published on Tuesday 23rd February 2016

---

*Saturday 13th February - League Two*

### Portsmouth 3    Bristol Rovers 1

Evans - 19', Smith - 45 +3',    Brown - 90 +1'
McNulty - 77'

**Rovers:** Mildenhall, Leadbitter, Lockyer [Booked], Parkes, Brown [Booked], Lawrence (Lines - 77'), Sinclair, Mansell (Montaño - 55' [Booked]), Bodin, Easter [Booked] (Taylor - 55'), Gaffney.

*Unused Substitutes:* Puddy, McChrystal, O Clarke, Fallon.

Attendance: 17,808 inc 2,863 Gasheads

Referee: Trevor Kettle (3rd time this season)

---

*Saturday 20th February - League Two*

### Bristol Rovers 2    Morecambe 1

Gaffney - 68', Bodin - 78'    Devitt - 12' (pen)

**Rovers:** Mildenhall, Leadbitter, J Clarke (Bodin - 32'), Lockyer, Parkes, Brown [Booked], Lawrence, Lines (O Clarke - 90'), Sinclair, Taylor (Easter - 78'), Gaffney.

*Unused Substitutes:* Puddy, McChrystal, Fallon, Montaño.
Attendance: 7,400 inc 92 Shrimps

Referee: Darren England

---

### ⊗   In recent Rovers news   ⊗

Not a lot again. Oh, except a long awaited 'clean' takeover of Rovers flying out of left field! The Jordanian Al-Qadi family, founders of the Arab Jordan Investment Bank, bought 92% of our club, sweeping all the local businessmen aside in one foul swoop. Mr Wael Al-Qadi became President and installed Steve Hamer (former Swansea City chairman) as the new Chair of the Board of Directors.

As all the best Jordan puns and spoonerisms have already been used I have given up trying and turned instead to Timbuk3's mis-understood 1986 single. I had toyed with a memory of 'Petra' the Blue Peter dog, tried in vain to make Hashemite rhyme with something other than Vegemite, and almost plumped for a mash-up of the awful 70's group Showaddywaddy.

The news of the Al-Qadi takeover broke a few days ago and it has been a whirlwind of interviews and opinions ever since. The timing is of course curious, whilst a major court appeal is in deliberation, but the timing proba-bly matters not. And at the risk of sounding melodramatic, the other notable news of the week was a narrow 2-1 win over mid-table Morecambe.

The latter may not sound important now but at 1-0 down and with barely a shot at goal to silence a twitchy crowd, that was the most pressure Darrell Clarke had been under for quite some time, and with so many rivals in good form a loss would have left us in tenth place and anxiety building rapidly.

It is early days yet, but the takeover does seem very positive, and hopefully the titular shades really will be needed for the bright sun rather than a Cold War nuclear apocalypse. You can hardly asset strip a club with significant debts and a contract of sale that has been quashed by a High Court judge. And the playing budget probably can't get much lower than it has been for the past two seasons

I realise I get energised each time planning permission has been granted on a new or redeveloped stadium (yes, I must be easily excitable…), but this time it really does seem like we might be able to get our facilities in order, whatever the result of the Sainsbury's case. Even if all that happens in the next few years is a debt-free club building a spanking new stadium with excellent transport links, that would be an amazing result for our future.

I won't think too much further than that at the moment, as on the pitch success is not as easy as infrastructure projects are, but on that side of the fence there is surely also a decent chance we can at least get back to our average historic level, namely the top half of League One.

As I have regularly mentioned in my articles, it has been tough having the planning permission in our pocket for the past three years but not the money, and to be reminded regularly that the shortfall is a relatively trifling amount in the world of modern football. Indeed, it has been sickening to see transfer fees for mediocre Premier League players regularly topping what we would need to build a beautiful new stadium, or to witness our neighbours blissfully losing around £10m a year whilst we scratch around for corn in the chicken coop.

Gasheads are not asking for Man City-esque cash, but we would like a stadium and training / academy facilities fit for the 20th Century, let alone the 21st. Matt Macey, Alfie Santos, Donovan Wilson and many others didn't move on (before even seeing out their teenage years) solely for the money, but also for the perceived chances of longer term success, and the general discernment that higher clubs have better coaches, better facilities and even better medical treatment when injured (the latter point should not be under-estimated).

Whilst I'm not so naïve to think that a new stadium and hopefully better facilities guarantees success, I do think it gives you a basis for potentially SUSTAINING any footballing success that can be attained. Facilities do mean a lot to a footballer, the back room staff, and even a manager.

Rovers stalwart, Ray Kendall, related in his memoirs, 'An Away Game Every Week' (*Breedon Books - 2001*), the story of how Martin O'Neill turned down the chance to leave non-league Wycombe Wanderers (who had recently moved to the small but brand new Adams Park in 1990) to manage Rovers in what is now entitled the Championship. Kendall recalls being introduced to the ex-Nottingham Forest Champions League double winner in the shadows of the Portakabins at the training 'facilities' at Fry's chocolate factory.

The ex-Northern Ireland captain turned to Ray and asked "Is this where you normally train?", and after being told yes, mused, "No, I don't think I could swap this for the luxury I have got at Wycombe". And that was that. Just over two years later he joined newly relegated Norwich City, in the Champi-onship.

History may well be kind to Nick Higgs, despite two relegations. A clean, media-free, takeover to a wealthy family with a football infatuated member seems to be a slap in the face to the numerous Internet naysayer's who mischievously foretold Rovers going into administration, and who perceived that a lack of information meant a lack of activity.

The bottom line is that no business, even a community based asset like a football club, really does its business out in the open, and those who think it will might as well wake up and smell the coffee. Many also giggled at Higgs embarking on a front page 'come and get us' interview for a Bahraini-based newspaper in January 2015.

Overall it seems positive that there has been a clean sweep of the business-men on the old Board. However, if Nick Higgs could potentially be a benevolent dictator when owning 54% of the shares, imagine what owning 92.6% of the club must be like. It does make you wonder what Board meetings may look like now. Will it be just Steve Hamer, as the representative of Wael Al-Qadi, and Lee Atkins (whoever he is...), sitting around an enormous table with the so-called fan's directors Ken Masters and Brian Seymour-Smith?

In some respects that is rather worrying, as is the general lack of other voices at a high level, but whilst I have no inclination for Rovers to get top heavy with staff, or be in a situation where a tail of powerful employees seem to be waging the dog, the positive outcome could be an increase in professional paid employees rather than Board members attempting to lead on numerous themes.

I was genuinely shocked recently when Bolton Wanderers were reported as not being able to afford to pay their 300+ staff. My shock was not at their well documented money worries, but by the level of staff! I doubt we would muster 20% of that.

I pray that the takeover will ensure the UWE stadium gets built, and lead to a revolution (not evolution) in training and academy facilities, and I pray that the new President is genuinely as bright and sincere as he sounds so far.

Surely all Gasheads can say Amman to that.

# the games people play

### published on Friday 26th February 2016

⊗ **In recent Rovers news** ⊗

Rounding off the takeover news... Ex-Chairman and majority share-holder Nick Higgs, along with board members Barry Bradshaw, Chris Jelf and Ed Ware are all created Life Vice Presidents. Ex-Board members Geoff Dunford and Rod King followed suit a short time after.

When I started writing this article about 10 days ago, I began by postulating that after the Accrington Stanley defeat and an empty weekend due to the rain, the League Two table now had a more realistic feel to it, as although we slipped to fifth only four teams in the top 10 now had games in hand on us. This re-alignment was nothing to worry about and was hardly a surprise as even when we were fourth in the published table, the 'true table' (i.e. average points per game played) usually put us sixth.

If Joe South's 1968 smash hit 'Games People Play' was, like Dr. Eric Berne's seminal psychology book of the same name, about human relationships and the chess-like transactions between them, then the League Two table was all about complex clashes amongst the top teams and games played (or not played, as the case may be...).

But defeat for Rovers at Pompey (we haven't won there since 1975), and several wins for rivals, slid us down the back of a slippery snake into eighth whilst our opponents catapulted up a nice ladder, and the article was surely in need of a re-write.

Or was it?

Rather like not entering the relegation zone until the final 54 minutes of the entire nine month long season, being in or out of any 'zone' is often more about psychology than hard cold logic, and unfortunately many teams don't take relegation seriously until actually under that dreaded dashed line. It would, for example, have done us good to have dipped our toe in the icy water of relegation earlier in 2014 as it would have seen us take the threat of the hangman's noose more seriously and may have launched Operation Survival rather than see us stumble on with Operation We've Too Much History To Go Down, as if we really didn't have a clue. Doh!

Staying in the play-off zone between December and February is a charade really. Of course it was great to be there, and of course it was really disappointing to have fallen out of it, but there are always plenty of frosty draughts that can hit you when you are near the top of any sporting division; what matters is that you don't actually catch a raging cold or lose your marbles.

No-one has a monopoly on success and success can't truly be measured until the last fixture of a season when everyone has played 46 games. By that point caring about the size, name, history or fashionableness of a club is merely a trivial pursuit. The final table does not lie.

Thinking of the word 'unfashionable' surely only the most stubborn defender of the indefensible would fail to envisage Accrington Stanley staying in the top seven, or even reaching the top three. They haven't been out of the top eight since mid-September and it was only their three games in hand that keep them below us for a while.

I think we could still manage to stay into the zone, and although the patch of games against the top teams has been disappointing so far, we have a few more in which to redeem ourselves, plus a lot of contests against lesser opposition.

I am not yet convinced by Mansfield Town, as they are the holders of a truly bizarre statistic of not having beaten any team in the top 14 (drawn 8, lost 10), but having gobbled up every opponent, bar one, in the bottom eight like a pack of hungry hippos (won 14, drawn 1, lost 0). They still have time to change of course, but any team who fail to beat those around them rarely achieve promotion. If I'm proven to be wrong on this I'll hold my hands up and say sorry!

When I started writing this piece I had AFC Wimbledon down as a promising wild card, but you don't have to be a mastermind to now see them as a bona fide promotion contender. They've won seven out of their eight games since our lethargic Boxing Day stalemate (it seemed that day as if the players had eaten rather too many leftovers from that joint of back gammon) and have scored at least a brace in all bar their most recent match.

So guess who that leaves as my sole risky outsider? Carlisle United have been up and down like a yo-yo this season (as high as fifth and as low as 20th), but may be able to bridge the gap to the top seven, and following the Cumbrians could never be described as dull as battleship grey.

I have written several times about mini-crises under Darrell Clarke, and maybe this sticky patch has been a new one to face. The vital win over Morecambe and a few opportune results elsewhere has seen us scrabble back into a play-off slot whilst only a solitary club in the top 11 now has a game in hand on us, and indeed we now hold a game or two in hand against half a dozen of the others.

Having whetted the appetite of Gasheads, especially the more casual ones, the pressure is now on to stay in the top seven rather than topple over like a line of dominoes.

Yes, another secret word search, this time inspired by the title of the article, with 26 'games' hidden in the piece. They are mainly traditional board games and physical games, but it does also include a few card and electronic games:

2nd paragraph - Chess
3rd para - Snakes & Ladders (well... almost!), Catapult
5th para - Hangman, Operation, Go, Cluedo (my favourite insertion)
6th para - Charades, Draughts, Catch, Marbles, Monopoly, Trivial Pursuit
7th para - Defender
9th para - Hungry Hippos, Sorry!
10th para - Cards, Mastermind, Backgammon
11th para - Guess Who?, Risk, Yo-Yo, Bridge, Battleship
12th para - Scrabble
13th para - Dominoes

&#x265B; ABOVE - Oscar Lewis and his amazing performing thumbs at the Rovers Open Day (Photo by Mark Lewis)

&#x265B; LEFT - Nick Day interviewing Oscar at the Rovers Open Day in July 2015 (Photo by Mark Lewis)

&#x265B; BOTTOM LEFT - Tam Johnson at AFC Wimbledon with Haydon the Womble during her quest to get a photo with every mascot in Western Europe. Earlier in 2015 Haydon famously crowd surfed when the Dons were giving Liverpool a run for their money. The things men will do for fame... (Photo by David Johnson)

&#x265B; BOTTOM RIGHT - Tam Johnson with Spytty the Dog, the rather dubious Newport County AFC mascot. I'm not entirely convinced that his huge flapping tongue is appropriate, even taking into consideration the Spit the Dog inspiration (Photo by David Johnson)

☠ TOP - Rovers warming up in front of one man and his monkey at Hartlepool United in September 2015. Many consider this match to be the turning point of the season (Photo by Alan Long)

☠ ABOVE - The surfer flag on the North Terrace before the Mansfield Town game in March 2016 (Photo by Rich Clark)

☠ LEFT - Brand new President Wael al-Kadi gets stopped for another selfie at the Morecambe game, the day after his family took control of BRFC (Photo by Rick Weston)

✂ TOP - Captain Gas at the Cambridge United match on Good Friday, complete with dreads and Hoxton hipster beard, in front of the deliciously elegant 'Make us Dream' flag (Photo by Martin Bull)

✂ BOTTOM - The crowd on the Blackthorn left happy after the narrow 1-0 karma defeat of Mansfield Town in March 2016 (Photo by Chris Bull)

## SPECIAL FEATURE - A DAGENHAM & REDBRIDGE TIMELINE

☠ TOP - 13.38pm - The calm before the storm - John Sweet, Amelie Ford & Irene Ford are among the first in the Mem. It was Irene's first Rovers match since the 70s at Eastville  (Photo by Steve Ford)

☠ BOTTOM - 16.48pm - Mayhem after Browner's right foot puts in the late, late goal  (Photo by Rick Weston)

♟  TOP - 16.54pm - DC looks in total shock.  Well, wouldn't you be when grasped around the neck by a large, sweaty, half-naked, bald stranger?  (Photo by Rick Weston)

♟  BOTTOM - 16.54pm - 'Hallelujah' from one Gashead as the promotion news filters through  (Photo by Rick Weston)

♟ TOP LEFT - 16.54pm - Wayne Collins, Gary Collins and Charley celebrate ANOTHER promotion  (Photo by Wayne Collins)

♟ TOP RIGHT - 17.00pm - Stewards guard the infamous post that Matty Taylor hit before rebounding to Browner.  The identity of the pasty eating steward has been concealed to protect a hungry man.  We can all relate to that.  (Photo by Martin Bull)

♟ BOTTOM - 17.01pm - Young lovers share a promotion kiss. Let's hope they were supposed to be in that position!  (Photo by Martin Bull)

⚽ TOP LEFT - 16.50pm - Lee Brown does his 'lez be 'avin yoooou' impersonation after his goal  (Photo by Rick Weston)

⚽ TOP FAR RIGHT - Steve Collett & daughter Gracie  (Photo by Steve Collett)

⚽ MIDDLE RIGHT - 17.02pm - No promotion would be complete without a random inflatable sheep  (Photo by Martin Bull)

⚽ BOTTOM - 17.22pm - Well, that's one way to celebrate. And it'll be on social media in seconds  (Photo by Rick Weston)

✗ TOP - 17.32pm - Dreams can come true if you pay homage to the foppish Pirate (Photo by Martin Bull)

✗ LEFT - 18.34pm - The excitement has been all too much for our boy wonder Oscar (Photo by Mark Lewis)

✗ RIGHT - We end the photos where they began, albeit one year later, at the Rovers Open Day for 2016. No Open Day would be complete without rain, or a first ever visit to the Mem. Today it was the turn of 19 day old Emily Clark, with wet mum and dad, Vicki and Rich. The things wife's do for love! (Photo by Rich Clark)

# priced out - reloaded

### published on Friday 4th March 2016

---

*Saturday 27th February - League Two*

## Wycombe Wanderers 1      Bristol Rovers 0

O'Nien - 85'

**Rovers:** Mildenhall, Leadbitter (Bodin - 57'), J Clarke [Booked], Lockyer, Mc-Chrystal [Booked], Brown, Lawrence [Booked] (Fallon - 87'), O Clarke, Mansell, Easter (Taylor - 67'), Gaffney [Booked].

*Unused Substitutes:* Puddy, Montaño. Parkes, Lines.

Attendance: 4,759 inc 1,629 Gasheads

Referee: Chris Sarginson (2nd time this season)

---

*Tuesday 1st March - League Two*

## Bristol Rovers 4      Hartlepool United 1

Taylor - 10', 38' & 56',      Paynter - 52'
Gaffney - 31'

**Rovers:** Mildenhall, J Clarke, Lockyer, McChrystal [Booked], Brown, Lawrence, Mansell (O Clarke - 83'), Lines, Bodin, Taylor (Easter - 75'), Gaffney (Harrison - 78').

*Unused Substitutes:* Puddy, Montaño. Parkes, Leadbitter.

Attendance: 6,634 inc 87 well travelled Monkey Hangers

Referee: Lee Swabey (2nd time this season)

---

### ⊗   In recent Rovers news   ⊗

☠ Jake Gosling hopped over the Severn for a one month refresher loan at Newport County AFC, whilst young 'un Jay Malpas did similar in an Easterly direction, to Chippenham Town.

☠ Kieran Preston went on loan to Rushall Olympic until the end of the season, plugging an urgent gap in The Pics back line.  Olympic presumably got their novel nickname from many decades earlier when most locals worked at the nearby Aldridge Colliery.

Sadly any positives that could have come out of my article published here just over a month ago, entitled 'Priced Out', seems to have been overtaken by the takeover. Whilst I believe the takeover has been very positive overall, it is a shame that the timing will help create the lowest home attendances seen for a long time.

The Board of Directors, via the kind offer of Brian Seymour-Smith, one of the Supporters Clubs Directors to the Board, were due to look at some of the issues in my article, but delays and then a certain spot of business scuppered that.

With three home games in 12 days, including the peculiar congested timing of our only two evening games at the Mem between the 1st of December and the end of the season, fans are feeling it in their pockets and the club have done nothing to alleviate the strain.

Before anyone reminds me that a certain take-over has (rightly) taken centre stage recently, as a Board member of several organisation's myself I would state that quick simple decisions can be made in community orientated organisation's when the will exists, and if they cannot then the organisation needs to rapidly look at its governance and decision making structure.

The amount of paying fans on these evenings will be very low, and a large amount of our capacity will remain empty. If the Plymouth Argyle game had the perfect calm to attract a bumper showing from both sets of fans, then games against Hartlepool United and AFC Wimbledon, when in a mini-slump, with an early Easter looming, and straight after five well attended away games since New Year (an average away following of 1,731 Gasheads at an average journey of 243 miles from Bristol), are the perfect storm the other way.

The attendance for Pools was indeed the fifth lowest home League gate of the season so far.

Around the New Year Rovers rode on a crest of a wave and enjoyed a chain of circumstances that almost guaranteed high crowds. But the club rather got carried away with the money making opportunities of those few weeks and failed to show any concern about the number of games coming up. The crowds that averaged 9,719 for those three games are now back to a more natural level of 6,000 - 7,500 and gaps are very clearly visible again.

What a shame the gaps aren't being filled by Gasheads, people who might become Gasheads or even just people who want to watch a game of real, live football, how it was meant to be experienced.

Season ticket holders always seem to be happy, but not everyone can commit themselves to a season ticket, or afford it, and the lack of incentives for non-season ticket holders for these two evening games in particular has been a real missed opportunity.

I have been a season ticket holder in the past and I know that it is good value for money and offers other benefits, such as priority on scarce away tickets, so I certainly won't be grouchy about that, but I am disappointed at the attitude of some of our season ticket holders, who are resistant to any offers that they see as negating their 'investment' and sometimes are very unsympathetic to fellow supporters who cannot attend every game.

This attitude in life is what keeps the insipid status quo grinding on relentlessly, and the haves looking down at the have-nots.

Football fans need to stick together, not get pulled apart. We are all Gasheads, just with different life journeys, salaries, geography and commitments.

An early bird Season Ticket for an adult on the Blackthorn Terrace was £260. If a fan bought an individual early bird ticket in person (i.e. without incurring booking or postage charges; more on those later...) for every League match of the season it would cost £392 this season. That situation is of course unlikely, but it is used to give some impression to season ticket holders that you have nothing to fear from an occasional game by game ticket 'offer' from the club, be it for adults or just as importantly for kids (my brother for one has asked me several times what matches could be 'quid a kid' - my reply has been noticeably silent for an entire season).

Your support towards what is often disparaging labelled 'casual fans' would be appreciated.

A more reasonable scenario could be a fan using the rather bureaucratic five or ten game flexi-ticket, which would work out at £346 for the season. At the other end of the scale, if an adult was wacky enough to roll up and pay on the gate to every game it would set them back an eye-watering £426. I will only give this one example, not because there are smaller disparities in other areas of the Mem, but because that terrace has the peak population of Pirates and since there simply isn't the space or time to look at every permutation.

I have no political agenda; I just want Gasheads of all financial persuasions to be able to watch some League matches this season at a reasonable price, for irregular supporters with kids to get a fair deal, and in the short term to scrap the ludicrous Category A status of the forthcoming games against Exeter City and Yeovil Town, those massive rivals with huge hooligan crews. If sarcasm really is the lowest form of wit, I plead guilty your honour. It's often the only medium left when nothing is changing.

Then in the closed season the whole structure should be looked at, especially the fact that 26% of home games were designated as Category A this season, which adds £4 to most tickets, and that the student discount was scrapped in a city with one of the largest student populations in Britain.

Not all Rovers supporters live or work near enough the Mem or Kingswood to be able to buy tickets in person, so it is disappointing for exiles that the charges involved in buying an early bird ticket by phone or Internet almost negate the £2 saving.

Many other leisure activities offer no booking fees and free 'print at home' ticketing, including Gloucestershire County Cricket Club, only a generous slogged six down the road. I assume we cannot as we don't have bar code scanners at the Mem; yet another reason to want the UWE built ASAP.

Gasheads were roundly applauded for sticking with the club when in non-league. It's a shame we weren't rewarded for it.

# good morning mr. magpie, can we play you every week?

### published on Saturday 12th March 2016

---

*Saturday 5th March - League Two*

### Notts County  0    Bristol Rovers  2

Montaño - 43', Brown - 50'

**Rovers:** Mildenhall, J Clarke, Lockyer, McChrystal, Brown, Lawrence (Montaño -3'), Mansell, Lines (O Clarke - 85'), Bodin, Taylor, Easter (Fallon - 88').

*Unused Substitutes:* Puddy, Parkes, Leadbitter, Broom.

Attendance: 5,052 inc 1,108 Gasheads

Referee: Tim Robinson

---

*Tuesday 8th March - League Two*

### Bristol Rovers  3    AFC Wimbledon  1

Easter - 28', O Clarke - 38',    Meades - 52'
Taylor - 78'

**Rovers:** Mildenhall, Leadbitter (Montaño - 90 + 3'), J Clarke, Lockyer, Parkes, Brown,
O Clarke, Mansell (McChrystal - 84'), Lines, Taylor, Easter (McBurnie - 59').

*Unused Substitutes:* Puddy, Harrison, Fallon, Broom.

Attendance: 7,778 inc 303 of the REAL Dons

Referee: Ben Toner (2nd time this season)

---

### ⊗  In recent Rovers news  ⊗

Young Swansea City striker Oliver McBurnie joined on loan until the end of the season. Sharp brained Pirates may remember him scoring a sweet header for Chester at the Mem last season during their 5-1 hammering.

I must admit that even my (almost) unshakeable faith in Darrell Clarke was slightly unsettled during our recent run of five points in five games, with only four goals scored, and most importantly grave defeats to play-off rivals Accrington Stanley, Portsmouth & Wycombe Wanderers. That poor sequence may still come back to haunt us, but at least DC stopped the rot, as he always seems to manage, with three comfortable wins, nine goals, and teams like Notts County suggesting there are some dire bottom feeders left to play.

Tuesday's win against a Wimbledon team with pace, power and passing, especially upfront, and without an away loss since October, was particularly pleasing, and reclaimed some faith that we can maybe mix it with the better teams in the division. It has also topped off a quite remarkable turn around in home League results, with 22 points from the last eight games at the Mem replacing the dismal seven points from our first nine games.

We do still have a 'problem' though, in that our record against the best teams in the league is poor, with just nine points in 11 games against the current top seven sides, and the stat can't get that much better as we only have one team in the top nine left to play, and they are the Cobblers, in their own backyard.

I'm not sure if the statistics bear me out but it would be fair to expect that teams who reach the play-offs with poor records against their fellow play-off contenders could struggle. Of course we'll just have to cross that bridge if we come to it, and remind ourselves that last season our play-off success was built on current form and gelling as a team rather than a good record against our play-off rivals (only six points from six clashes).

At this time of the season the real judge of the forthcoming opposition is often more about their form than their position in the table. The bad news is therefore that forthcoming clashes with Newport County and Yeovil Town may be far harder than the table suggests, but the good news is that we have four others down there yet to play and Notts County clearly showed us that there are some truly pitiful teams in the depths who are in bad form and who won't be surfacing for air anytime soon. Our comfortable victory against Hartlepool United doesn't really fit either category as although their defence looked shambolic against us, they held runaway leaders Northampton Town in their previous game, and last Saturday became only the fifth team of the season to take three points away from the Hive, and the only one from the bottom half of the table.

The added wild card is that from Easter onwards we will start seeing some really desperate clubs scrabbling around at the bottom of the table getting genuinely concerned. Sometimes these teams hit remarkable form; other times they wilt like petrol station flowers.

Notts County could well be one of the rabble, shamelessly trading on their status as a founder member of the Football League in 1888, as if their history won't let them go down. Well, we certainly know all about that sort of attitude don't we? Excuse me if I have little sympathy for their puffed up club after the dirty battles of the late 80's / early 90's and the legendary 'ungentlemanly conduct' episode in September 2000, which although early in the season, could be seen as the stolen brace of points that eight months later saw us relegated, by a solitary point, to the Fourth Division for the first time in our history.

Karma has helped us to four wins out of five at Meadow Lane since that unsavoury episode, and last Saturday's win sounded like a pretty comfortable experience, which can hardly be said about Jamie Fullerton's managerial chair at the moment. There are times in life when unchecked 'ambition' fosters bad decision making, and given that Fullerton has had five football jobs in less than five years since joining Rovers in the summer of 2011 as Youth Team Coach (and leaving a year after), and has made some rather vocal critics in his playing and coaching career, this could well be one of those times.

Football fans apportion great credence to loyalty, and neither jumping from club to club, nor crossing the Trent from Forest to County, is much of a vote winner. Every manager in Britain knows there are certain poisonous jobs and boardroom dungeons that probably aren't worth striving for, at any salary, and the County hot seat must surely be up there alongside the rotten ducking stools at Villa Park, and that other tiding of self-important magpies in the North East.

It seems like the old superstition that a magpie is bad luck could be true, so instead of meeting a *pica pica* with the traditional greeting, "Good morning Mr. Magpie. How is your lady wife today?", healthier advice may be to run a country mile if 'Mike Ashley' or 'Ray Trew' ever pops up on a list of missed callers.

# automatic for the people

## published on Wednesday 16th March 2016

---

*Saturday 12th March - League Two*

### Bristol Rovers 1    Mansfield Town 0

Taylor - 61'

**Rovers:** Mildenhall, J Clarke, Lockyer, McChrystal, Brown [Booked], Montaño, Mansell [Booked], Lines (O Clarke - 84'), Bodin, Taylor (Harrison - 87' [Booked]), Easter (McBurnie - 62' [Booked]).

*Unused Substitutes:* Puddy, Leadbitter, Parkes, Broom.

Attendance: 7,847 inc 241 Stags

Referee: Dean Whitestone

---

⊗  **In recent Rovers news**  ⊗

☠ Rovers fans are still talking about the biggest news to hit the Mem since Danny Coles tried to fight his own shadow; a new scoreboard! Electronic as well, and boasting a circa 1987 'GOAL' graphic. Tip top.

☠ The Mansfield game marked DC's 100th game in charge of Rovers.

---

After a perfect March so far, hitting the heady heights of fourth, and seeing other teams slip up this weekend, it has suddenly come as a bit of a shock that we are now in touching distance of the automatic promotion slots. In fact it's quite startling, especially as I remember how we made League Two look so difficult for eight and a half previous seasons out of nine, whilst clubs like Crawley Town, Hartlepool United (twice), Mansfield Town, Rochdale, Rushden & Diamonds (remember them?), Shrewsbury Town, Torquay United, and Wrexham made escape from the bottom look relatively simple.

Yes, the above names are true; they really were amongst the clubs gaining automatic promotion between 2001-2007 or 2011-2014. Play-off winners included two more towns; Cheltenham and Fleetwood. Meanwhile in the city of Bristol we made going up look as difficult as putting a man on the moon; our average finish was 15th.

In archetypal Gashead fashion I've been trying not to think about the top three, after being bitten too many times by the disappointment bug in the past. In addition, the triumvirate of Plymouth Argyle, Oxford United and Northampton Town have been continuously camped above the dotted line since 14th November, and until last weekend it looked like they could well squat there and try not to breathe until the end of the season.

Although I had noticed chinks in the usually robust hide of Oxford United (merely the 11th best home record in the League, including defeats to four of the current top seven), I am rather more surprised to see Argyle a lowly 15th in the form table for the last 10 games and surely now a team that could potentially be caught. This is no time of the season to be having a wobble with any more longevity than a mere blip (© Oscar Wilde 1891, or was it Martin Bull 2016?).

As the top seven have played nearly all of their games against each other, the League will be decided on who can cope the best against the middling and struggling teams, how they deal with the injuries that tend to accumulate at this time of the season, plus any suspensions, and, perhaps most importantly, what reserves of experience, drive and mental strength they hold.

It truly is a squad game now, and it's encouraging to see irregular players like Mark McChrystal, Ollie Clarke and Cristian Montaño having some of their best games of the season; indeed Monty got a raw deal when a formation change led to him being dropped after a MOTM performance at Notts County.

A sudden spate of Pirate injuries, thankfully most relatively minor, is an uncommon hurdle for Darrell Clarke to overcome as we hit the 10 match run-in to the end of the season. We had previously been remarkably blessed by a lack of damage, with only Will Puddy's groin really upsetting the apple cart. We also hold a noteworthy record of not losing even a single player to suspension so far this season, with no bans for accumulated yellows, and both the red cards that were wafted in our direction were rescinded on appeal. In comparison it was easy to see on Saturday why Mansfield Town have the worst disciplinary record in the League.

However, we currently have two key players out (Stuart Sinclair and Rory Gaffney), and others out or at the edge of their bodily limits; nearly everybody hurts at this late stage of a long season. And the Easter weekend will see an unusual situation thump us, in that Ellis Harrison, Oliver McBurnie, and most significantly Tom Lockyer, will be away on International duty but we won't be allowed to postpone the games. I can envisage several journo's already warming up the cliché bus, with 'down to the bare bones' and 'kids on the bench'.

☻

Meanwhile, back on the pitch Rovers calmly dispatched Mansfield Town by the karmic score line of 1-0. Indeed for those out there touched by the train spotter stick there was a delicious symmetry to DC gaining his 50th win in his 100th match as Rovers manager. Matty Taylor also poached his 20th goal of the season (he leads League Two for goals from inside the six yard box, with eight so far), and Rovers already have more points this season than we achieved in all our other League Two campaigns except the promotion season of 2006/7 (we are only 10 points away though).

As usual though football commentators tend to focus on the limitations of the opposition rather than the patience shown by our own team, with analysis regularly focusing on the Stags lack of sharp antlers up top. Whilst it's certainly true they came for a point and (just) left with nothing, I'd take that as a compliment rather than use it to berate Mansfield. It's something we could have been accused of not that long ago, and is often not a tactic as such, but a simple realisation that one team isn't as good as the other.

Rovers are gelling more as a team, and our solidity and mutual understanding is what will probably force more and more teams to come to the Mem looking for a draw, and live life on the break. It's a perennial problem in football, and the reason we find it hard to slice through these teams like a hot knife through butter is precisely because we are a League Two team. If we had the creativity and goal scoring prowess to make wins look easy we wouldn't be in this division.

Maybe by the end of May we won't be? Or even by early May?

Why not dream of automatic promotion for the people. It costs nothing.

This article was named after R.E.M.'s 1992 album 'Automatic for the People'.

Rather by accident (I'm not even a R.E.M. fan), I started seeing if the song titles could be used in the text. I managed almost half of the tracks before running out of time:

2nd paragraph - Man on the Moon; 3rd para - Try Not to Breathe; 5th para - Drive; 6th para - Monty Got a Raw Deal; 8th para - Everybody Hurts.

# golden brown

### published on Tuesday 22nd March 2016

---

*Saturday 19th March - League Two*

### Newport County AFC  1    Bristol Rovers  4

Rodman - 2'      O Clarke - 15', Montaño - 55',
                 Taylor - 61', Harrison - 85'

**Rovers:** Mildenhall, J Clarke, Lockyer, McChrystal, Brown,
Montaño (Broom - 85'), Lines, O Clarke, Bodin,
Taylor (Harrison - 75' [Booked]), Gaffney (McBurnie - 58').

*Unused Substitutes:* Puddy, Leadbitter, Parkes, Easter.

Attendance: 3,663 inc 1,042 Gasheads

Referee: Graham Salisbury (2nd time this season)

---

### ⊗  In recent Rovers news  ⊗

☠ Newport born Ellis Harrison smashes the final goal in the 4-1 tonking of his home town club, and fellow Newportonian Ryan Broom made his League debut as sub. They follow a long line of Gas from the town, including Tony Pulis and Byron 'The Lord' Anthony.

---

The Stranglers' lead singer Hugh Cornwell is a regular sight in and around the Bath and Bristol area. Given that 'Golden Brown', their highest chart hit in 1982 was about heroin, it's not totally surprising that its most frequently misheard lyric could maybe be explained by a subliminal expectation that the opening line "Golden Brown texture like sun, Lays me down with my mind she runs" would be more fitting if it really did end 'with my man-cheera', evoking some unsalubrious slang for a dodgy dalliance down the back alleys of Easton.

If Mr. Cornwell, a not very 'punk' alumnus of Bristol University, had periods of debauchery, incarceration and excess in his early life (his autobiography isn't entitled 'A Multitude of Sins' for nothing), the same cannot be said of our own Golden Brown, left back Lee Brown.

Mr. Brown seems to be an increasingly rare example of a young, modern day footballer who shuns the limelight and silly haircuts and just gets on with the job. No whinging, no bad discipline or silly fouls (only 14 yellow cards for Rovers and never a red), and no executive box urinations * or salacious rumours about his personal life. Fit, healthy, never injured, properly left footed, honest, and loyal; what more can a supporter want?

Lee also has an eye for the onion bag (18 gas goals so far), can execute excellent free kicks and corners, and can even take penalties, admittedly with varying success on that front. Given that he had missed his two previous pens, stepping up to be one of the first five takers at Wembley just about summed up the man's rock-solid character.

Lee has played a part in 226 games out of a maximum possible of 247 since being brought to us in June 2011 by the much maligned Paul Buckle, and apart from 'only' coming on as a sub for the F.A. Cup 3rd Round game against Aston Villa in January 2012 has played every minute of all 23 Cup games we've faced in our last five seasons. I hope he could reach 500 appearances for us. In fact him and Tom Lockyer (over 135 appearances at the age of 21) could be the only players for a very long time who may have even the merest sliver of a chance to better Stuart Taylor's all-time appearance record of 546 League games.

He's our only certified ever present of the season so far (i.e. started all League matches), one of a select band of only 15 players in League Two with the same record. He also possesses a statistic less easily recognised, namely being on the pitch for every minute of all those games. Only six others still cling to that extra accolade in League Two, and two of those are goalkeepers.

His squad leading nine assists for the 2013/14 season were the highest in the squad, far more than Michael Smith's trio from the other side, just like his nine more in non-league outshone Tom Lockyer and Daniel Leadbitter combined on the right hand flank, with only a brace between them. This season he's currently on five, with only Chris Lines ahead of him, on seven.

Limitations? Some Pirates still don't seem to rate him which I find quite bizarre. Maybe it's a Gashead trait to expect perfection from our current League Two players, yet fail to complain properly during the years we were full to bursting point with over-paid wasters on the books, or more likely, in the treatment room. If Browner was told to report to the physio, he'd probably innocently reply, 'who?'.

Every year Internet forums ask questions like 'where do we need to strengthen?' and several replies will ask for a left back to provide cover or competition for Browner. In a perfect world I could just about understand it, especially the competition angle, but surely when faced with limited budgets and spaces for players (EVERY player takes up valuable resources at a football club) people like Lee Brown are a godsend, as they really only require a youngster like Danny Greenslade who could cover for a few games if necessary. In fact having a senior player to cover for him would be like having an expensive second string centre-back behind Paolo Maldini; it almost guarantees that a squad member will be underplayed and under happy.

I can relate much more to a couple of minor weaknesses, namely that Lee is a little one-paced, not blessed with a real top speed, and whilst his lack of yellow cards is admirable, the sceptic would suggest it's because he's not a tough tackler, does not easily commit himself, and plays on his feet, rather than his bum. Whilst the latter is generally a positive trait, it could be regarded as a bit wimpy and some fans question his defensive capabilities.

I will certainly acknowledge some minor chinks in his armour, but would suggest that his defensive performance will often depend on the formation, the role he is asked to play and who is playing in front of him, and he'd still always be one of the first names on my team sheet.

There is never a frown with golden Brown.

* - Note - this refered to some unsavoury news that came out of Cheltenham races, where several footballers found themselves on the front pages of the tabloid press. Not totally surprisingly one from across the river was caught up in it.

# the future is bright, the future is clarke

## published on Thursday 24th March 2016

⊗ **Statto Alert - 2015/16 season** ⊗

Matty Taylor ended the season as the joint top scorer of headers in League Two, with six. Not bad for a little 'un. Only Jayden Stockley matched him, whilst on loan at Portsmouth and Exeter City.

Billy Bodin and Rory Gaffney were the joint second highest League Two goal scorers with their left peg. They had six each, alongside Jay Simpson (Leyton Orient) and Gary Roberts (Pompey). Plymouth's Graham Carey eclipsed them all with ten sinister strikes. With only one goal from his other foot it seems clear that his right leg is just for standing on.

If we asked Gasheads which player has the third highest number of League starts for Rovers this season, I doubt many would guess James Clarke, with 33, just a brace behind Tom Lockyer, and a further brace behind Lee 'Golden' Brown, the subject of my previous (relatively) 'unsung hero' article.

Gasheads don't seem to have taken James to their hearts yet, but I would ask quite what more we should expect from someone making his Football League debut at the ripe age of 25. James has been a virtual ever present as either the right hand man in a defensive three, or as a more traditional right back in a 4-4-2, and has been another excellent Darrell Clarke find (even if it is via the Salisbury connection).

Clarke has always struck me as an old fashioned right back, which may explain why his contribution has almost gone unnoticed. Not blessed with the height and strength of a bullying centre-back, or the pace and engine of a more modern right back or wing back, the lesser spotted Clarke is rarely observed over the half way line, and has never scored a goal in his profession-al career. He has to rely on positioning, a comfort on the ball rarely seen in lower league defenders, and a steadiness that wins few admirers in this age of training ground tricks and showy displays of one's means of life. This solidity could almost make him a new Steve Yates, although, with all due respect, he's unlikely to ever be in his league, as by the age of 23 'Scooter' was already playing in the Premier League.

If Aesop's tortoise proved that sometimes 'slow and steady wins the race', then Consistent Clarke and Golden Brown could well be the cornerstone of a successful season.

If you find yourself with time on your hands, an entire historic Rovers XI can be made from Clark's, and Clarke's, most of them in their correct positions. My favourite was Billy 'The Judge' Clark, so named because he spent so much time on the bench. Billy was actually a very competent player, and managed 248 league appearances in a decade as an almost one club man, but was exceptionally unfortunate to be playing at the same time as the aforementioned Steve Yates, still the best defender I've ever seen in a Rovers shirt, and Geoff Twentyman, who went on a staggering 163 game ever-present League run lasting from Boxing Day 1987 to 23rd August 1991.

The other Clarke I want to highlight is Ollie. A local lad who came through the youth system and whose 100th appearance for Rovers (a brief sub cameo at Notts County) seemed to go un-noticed. Although never a full regular like Lee Brown, or James Clarke, Ollie has now managed 70 starts, and come on 33 times as sub. His name-sake Darrell recently remarked, "I can't speak highly enough of Ollie. He's in and out of the team, yet he always gives me everything, every single day, in training".

The one thing that every watcher of Ollie will mention is a slightly silly haircut. Only joking... it's the long range cannonball shot he has. If Association Football was somehow like American Football and we could miraculously spirit him on when encountering a touch of space and a glimpse at goal, Ollie would the Most Valuable Player in many games.

Most of his eight goals in the blue and white quarters are memorable, but the two that top the pile for me are there for very different reasons.

The first was a bit of a speculative 25 yarder when no-one quite expected it, but his bending 55th minute strike against AFC Telford United in August 2014 proved to be the winner that day, and with it our first three point haul in non-league. It relieved the pressure on DC and vitally kept the home fans on board after two away defeats. Although Telford were later relegated they looked a respectable side in our encounters, and another Clarke strike in the return fixture (bizarrely only two months later; I think the Conference still have a Commodore 64 as their fixture computer) was again the only shot to separate the sides.

But in my top 1 is the instinctive 'worldie' that rescued a point for 10 man Rovers at Eastleigh, again in the 55th minute. This time it was at least 35 yards (it gets further away every time I think about it), and materialized from a wanton hash of a clearance from the usually reliable Spitfires goalie Ross Flitney. Lee Mansell helped win the ball for Clarke, and when Ollie saw the keeper wasn't quite back in position he lashed a boomerang-esque barnstormer into the postage stamp corner.

I was part of 1,000 Gasheads with a perfect view of it and that skinny metal terrace literally rocked off its hinges. It is up there with the best Rovers goals I've ever personally witnessed, and although a point at Eastleigh may sound distinctly pedestrian in the cold light of the League Two promotion spots, at the time it was a crucial comeback that proved we could handle adversity.

Ollie isn't just a shot machine, he's a tidy player who adheres to the 'keep it simple' philosophy, recycling the ball efficiently and tough tackling when needed. Slightly naïve at times, and in need of improved concentration, I suspect he can only improve, especially with the guidance of senior midfielders like Mansell and Chris Lines.

The future is bright, the future is Clarke.

# I wonder how the french say deja vu?

published on friday 1st April 2016, although the version below is an
expanded rendition that was finalized shortly after the original

---

*Good Friday 25th March - League Two*

### Bristol Rovers 3 Cambridge United 0

Bodin - 9' & 18', Taylor - 73'

**Rovers:** Mildenhall, Leadbitter, J Clarke, McChrystal, Brown, Montaño (Parkes - 74'), Lines, O Clarke (Lawrence - 72'), Bodin, Taylor, Gaffney (Easter - 79').

*Unused Substitutes:* Puddy, Fallon, Broom, Malpas.

Attendance: 10,262 inc 443 U's

Referee: Steve Martin (2nd time this season)

---

*Easter Monday 28th March - League Two*

### Carlisle United 3 Bristol Rovers 2

Stacey - 11', Wyke - 49', Bodin - 27', Taylor - 57'
Kennedy - 85'

**Rovers:** Mildenhall, J Clarke, Parkes [Booked], McChrystal, Brown, Montaño (Easter - 22'), Lines [Booked], O Clarke (Lawrence - 22'), Bodin, Taylor, Gaffney (Leadbitter - 82').

*Unused Substitutes:* Puddy, Fallon, Broom, Malpas.

Attendance: 4,718 inc 651 Gasheads

Referee: Darren England (2nd time this season)

---

### ⊗ Statto Alert ⊗

Until our visit to Cumbria Rovers had not lost a game this season where they had scored a brace or more. In fact we had previously won all 18 out of 18 such episodes. After the Carlisle United game Rovers scored two or more goals six more times, winning five of the matches and drawing one, thus giving an overall record of W23 D1 L1.

The moral of this story? Score goals!

The day before the start of this season I pondered what Gasheads could expect from a season back in League Two?

"I anticipate more of the same, with a tight-knit team improving as the season goes on, and staggered signings and loanee's coming and going to fill gaps. My heart says we could well continue our upward momentum, as many teams have done in the past, but my head reminds me that in nine previous seasons in 'the easiest League in the world to get out of' we had August optimism every season but reached the play-offs just once, and only finished in the top half of the table two other years, and they were both a statistic scrapping 12th".

My expectation was near enough what we have got, and happily the emotive 'heart' has won out over the worried 'head'.

The similarities between our two seasons with Darrell Clarke at the helm are startling.

Whilst rage still simmered over sleep walking to relegation in May 2014, a poor start in non-league got many Gasheads very twitchy indeed. Most remember the first eight days, with only a solitary point gained from a trio of matches, and then press fast forward to the loss at Braintree Town (where some fans were also disgraced), but have forgotten that sandwiched in between were crucial wins in both home games (including mugging the then leaders FC Halifax Town) and a dominant draw at Forest Green Rovers. Those seven points probably kept DC in a job.

Our lowest ebb may well have been an uninspiring 16th (call me old-school but in my childhood tables weren't even given for the first three games of the season), but after the humbling defeat at the Irons we lost only two more Conference matches in 42 encounters.

Rovers enjoyed an encouraging opening quartet of games this season, but then hit a sticky September with just a single point from five games, whilst reaching our nadir for the season (17th). However, we weren't completely to know at the time that all of those five clubs will most probably finish in the top eight of the League, and that our later rise would be so fast and so high that with seven games still left, we can't even mathematically finish any lower than that same number, 17th, and in reality a play-off berth already looks solid. Surely not even Ian Holloway could throw this position away?

By mid-December 2014 an eight match unbeaten run had squeezed us into second spot for the first time, but were still nine points and 24 goals behind runaway leaders Barnet. Although I had certainly not given up on the prospect of automatic promotion I did genuinely believe that we could win the FA Trophy as a fall-back for maybe not toppling Barnet.

One school of thought suggested that the Trophy can be a real distraction, but the previous season Cambridge United won it, via eight unbeaten games. Later in the season they also had three play-off games, and with a decent FA Cup run to boot, they played 60 games in a season. They did it successfully though, proving that winning is a habit, and a very nice one at that.

I was one of just 3,101 Rovers fans to witness the shock 2-0 home defeat to ex-landlords Bath City in the First Round of the said winnable trophy. Whilst the world and his Internet dog seemed to melt down all around me I frankly didn't care that much, and thought it was the jab of humility we needed to remind us that we were not going to crush all these non-leaguers in our glorious path; in fact we had been scrapping through games, had become the draw specialists of the league, and the quality of our squad and loanee's was about as shallow as Dorian Gray.

So, we knuckled down, won the next three league games, including coming back from behind twice against Gateshead, and went unbeaten until March.

This season's obligatory cup shock shouldn't therefore have been such a surprise, nor treated as such an unwelcome event. Although losing to Chesham United was in a way even worse (75 places below us in the pyramid), it did see the home hoodoo almost laid to rest, as the next game saw us manage only our second home win of the season (in our eighth game), and since the Tuesday night failure against Stevenage, the Mem has been the strongest fortress in the entire Football League, with 10 wins and a single draw.

Our second sticky streak this season occurred around the time of the reverse League fixtures, with just seven points in the seven games played from just after New Year's Day until the end of February.

We had a similar blip in non-league, but it occurred later, with only five points from the four March fixtures, which included a couple of insipid performances, the eventual dropping of Steve Mildenhall, and most importantly, relinquishing the top spot we temporarily held, but had never fully earned as Barnet always had a game in hand on us. We even slipped to third for a short time.

This season's March saw us finally stride forward with a confident swagger in our step, scoring 19 goals and looking like a real TEAM. Five of the six wins were by two goals or more, whereas in the previous 32 League games we achieved that level of dominance only six times. After 39 games we have 68 points, just six less than the same point last season.

Likewise last season the 1-0 grinds and the late winners were replaced in the Spring by dominant wins against Aldershot Town (3-1), Chester City (5-1), Kidderminster Harriers (3-0 away), Southport (2-0) and finally the 7-0 mauling of poor Alfreton Town. That all stood us in good stead to complete a hugely comfortable 3-0 aggregate play-off win against our so-called bogey side Forest Green Rovers, one of only two teams to win at the Mem in the regular season.

Oh, how far the Rovers had travelled in those nine months. And how the march has continued in the same style this time, despite minor stumbles along the path.

This is a really important aspect of how DC works. He moulds a team throughout the season, adding and subtracting, drilling the understanding home, consistently riding mini-slumps, and comes on strong towards the finish. It is little surprise that he has a perfect record in play-offs, having been in charge for a trio of post-season campaigns and emerged the winner of all three.

We've seen all this before, although in this League three teams get to go up automatically.

Could we?

Really?

# patience is a virtue
## published on Thursday 7th April 2016

---

*Saturday 2nd April - League Two*

### Bristol Rovers  3    Crawley Town  0

Taylor - 53' & 79', Lawrence - 75'

**Rovers:** Mildenhall, Leadbitter, Lockyer, McChrystal, Brown, Lawrence (Montaño - 77'), Lines [Booked], O Clarke, Bodin, Taylor (Easter - 85'), Gaffney (McBurnie - 83').

*Unused Substitutes:* Puddy, J Clarke, Parkes, Harrison.

Attendance: 8,250 inc 99 Red Devils

Referee: Fred Graham

---

### ⊗  In recent Rovers news  ⊗

☠ DC rightly wins League Two Manager of the Month for March. With 6 wins out of 7 it was surely a walkover.

☠ Matty Taylor wins League Two Player of the Month with an irresistible 8 goals in 7 games in March, including his second hat-trick of the season, a feat that was never matched by any other League Two player during the season.

---

As I watched Rovers slowly break through against a depressing Crawley Town side intent on subjecting paying supporters to a master class in anti-football, my brain ticked over with several matters.

At the frontal lobe was a feeling that some considerable patience could be needed today, both for supporters and players, and that we may need more of this heavenly virtue in the games remaining. As part of a terrace more often associated with wrath than patience, it was satisfying to see that the positivity of the past 18 months is slowly revealing itself in a more enduring attitude, & all because we finally have staff and players we can have faith in.

Although our form suggests that all of the 'six to go' are winnable, even at Northampton Town's Sixfields, history suggests there will be many twists and turns still left in this season. Although supporters of high flyers begin to consider themselves almost invincible, in reality there is invariably a Dover Athletic fly lurking in the ointment. And at 3.45pm on Saturday there were quite a few concerned that Crawley may yet creep away with the point they so coveted.

The whole point of a 46 game season is that it truly does decide who the best teams are, as the elite will be the most consistent at handling the myriad of situations thrown at them over the course of nine months; from heat to hail, injuries to terrible refs, dodgy penalties to quagmire pitches, and from expansive opponents to teams braying with leviathan donkeys. Patience and adaptability are often the keys to unlocking heaven's gate.

My **second** train of thought was how the 'English disease' has become the baby that has been unfairly thrown out with the bath water. No, I'm not talking about football hooliganism, but the idea promulgated by the so-called intelligentsia of football analysis, that the English love of a player who puts himself about is harming the game.

Whilst it is certainly true that decades ago the love of a grafter, a chaser of lost causes, or a 'get-stuck-inner', probably did hold too much sway, especially if the team was full of them, it is now equally unwise to go too far the other way. There is nothing wrong with players who hassle, harry and harass, who run the channels and make themselves available at every opportunity. To a team mate, especially the more lumpy ones, such an outlet is a godsend; a willing receptacle just waiting to be filled with football juice.

Every goal has a genesis, and in the beginning considerable effort is often needed in order to create the chance itself. Inferior managers will usually choose to ignore the back story though and just fumble around for the sound bite. On Saturday the hack's favoured lazy headline was that Rovers scored from three set-pieces, as if to suggest we are a military machine spending hours doing press-ups in the pouring rain.

Rovers' first goal was initially 'created' by Rory Gaffney's persistence and then his patient ball retention when little else was on. This lead to a corner, and from that corner we scored. The corner may have been a set piece, but if we had not won that corner it could never have been scored (I imagine Camus could have phrased this better than I am capable of).

These narrow margins can be the difference between success and failure, yet are scoffed at by those who preach that the best players should be effortlessly passing and walking the ball into the net.

Similarly some effort and retention from Ollie Clarke drew the foul which led to a plethora of talent queuing up to take a tasty free kick. It's great to have Chris Lines and Lee Brown ready to take a dead ball, and Lee Mansell on the sidelines, but it was a shrewd choice to let Liam Lawrence guide his sublime curler into the top corner. The ground erupted with relief at a comfortable cushion, at a time when our rivals were mainly winning.

And finally, a rasping shot from Cristian Montaño that almost capped off a slick move, barely seconds after stepping onto the pitch as a sub, earned us the corner that secured the third goal.

My **third** perception was how fortunate we are to finally be able to watch appealing football when we pay our hard earned cash to follow Rovers.

We aren't Barcelona, and we aren't always set up to be particularly expansive, but we do try to pass the ball, especially when confidence is high, and even when not having the greatest day at the office DC nearly always loosens the reins towards the end of the match and finishes with more creative players, trying to exploit tired legs and weary minds.

The Rovers we now see before us do at least try to entertain, and endeavour to win games, and this is bourn out by the dearth of draws this season, which can be counted on one hand. With six games left we are only four wins away from equalling our highest ever win tally in a season (26 in 1952/53 and 1989/90; interestingly our only two Champions titles), but can still equal our lowest quantity of draws in a 46 game season (Paul Trollope's five, in 2009/10). We've already scored more goals than in any Football League season since 2008/9, and been subjected to only two goalless fixtures.

The next patient project is Northampton Town and the positivity surrounding Rovers is so high that even if we dropped out of the top three again, our virtue would still remain with us.

# our greatest glory lies not in never having fallen, but in rising when we fall

### published on Tuesday 12th April 2016

---

*Saturday 9th April - League Two*

### Northampton Town  2    Bristol Rovers  2

Adams - 23', Hoskins - 49'    Taylor - 76', Harrison - 88'

**Rovers:** Mildenhall, Leadbitter [Booked], Lockyer, McChrystal, Brown, Lawrence (Montaño - 56'), Lines [Booked], O Clarke, Bodin (Easter - 71'), Taylor, Gaffney (Harrison - 56').

*Unused Substitutes:* Puddy, J Clarke, Parkes, Gosling.

Attendance: 7,579 inc 925 Gasheads

Referee: Tony Harrington

---

⊗    **In recent Rovers news**    ⊗

Stuart Sinclair receives the Football League Unsung Hero Award for March.

Whilst deciding how to write about the omnipotent one I elected to bow to the BRFC web site who summed it up elegantly when they wrote, "By the time the Bristol Rovers Community Department ask Stuart Sinclair to represent the club at an event, chances are he has already done it, put a smile on faces and left a lasting impression." All hail The Beard. Hip hip hooray!

---

Did the title of today's article emanate from Churchill's lips?

If not, maybe it was Gandhi? Buddha? Confucius? Wittgenstein?

Or even Eric 'ze seagulls follow ze trawler...' Cantona?

Not quite.

It's Hereford United's delightful motto, since passed down to its phoenix successor Hereford FC, whose manager is none other than Peter Beadle, who currently holds a staggering 85% win record with them.

And if anyone knows about falling and rising it must be Hereford. I have a soft spot for them, not just due to their nickname being my surname, and being a local club trying to survive in a rural area, but also as a consequence of a couple of wonderful visits there in recent years, one of which was in League One just seven seasons ago.

Hereford fans must have been in dream land in the mid-1970s as three promotions in five seasons saw them catapulted from non-league to the second tier for a solitary season. A double relegation dumped them back to the bottom tier but at least they were a Football League team, and they held onto that status for 19 more seasons.

They now play in the ninth tier, the Midland Football League Premier Division, alongside a plethora of delightfully named teams, including Quorn (a town in Leicestershire, not a fungus), Coventry Sphinx, Shepshed Dynamo (where Gerry Francis found Devon White playing, when named Shepshed Charterhouse), Continental Star, Dunkirk (Nottingham, not a French team trying to infiltrate our leagues), and Sporting Khalsa, the highest ranked Sikh club in Britain.

I almost expected Michael Palin's Barnstoneworth United to be on that list.

Whilst the prospect of an away game at Bardon Hill (population 26) may not be able to compete against the memory of the famous 1972 FA Cup Third Round defeat of Newcastle United which is re-run every year as a reminder of one of the biggest ever shocks in the oldest cup competition in the world, at least their loyal supporters still have a club, which is healthier than it looked in 2014 when their 90 years of existence ended in liquidation.

As for Rovers?

Well, the motto could almost be adopted for ourselves as after having fallen our own lowest ebb, and then rising again, Rovers have developed a resilience and determination rarely seen before. It may be a cliché but we really do not know when we are beaten. Gone are the days of insipid 'roll over and tickle my tummy' performances, when the first goal let in often became a second, heads drooped, and there was a collective lack of self-belief to stage any comeback.

When Gasheads pay their cash to watch their team they now know they'll never be able to leave early, from Barnet in the pouring rain in November

2014 to this weekend in front of a new record crowd at Sixfields. Rovers have scored 48 second half goals this season (the joint highest in League Two) and 18 of them have come in the last 10 minutes (the second highest).

At this point a multitude of stats could be wheeled out to showcase our rise after the inglorious fall. Last season included just one loss in the final 32 league and play-off matches (or two losses in 42 and play-off league matches; take your pick of stats), a 20 match unbeaten away run, and 24 clean sheets in 49 league and play-off games.

This season we are already only one more away victory from equalling our highest number of away wins in a season (11 in the 1989/90 Third Tier champions season - not a bad season to strive to follow), and have rescued 17 points so far from losing positions, the last one being at a runaway league leader who thought they were just about to celebrate a Championship.

One statistic in particular stands out a mile though and was one I didn't even realise until seeing it on the Internet. I knew that we had not been beaten this season when we had been the team to score first (in fact we've impressively won 17 out of 19 such occurrences, only very very late goals for Plymouth Argyle and Exeter City blotting our copybook) but what I did not realise was that we haven't lost at home from that situation since the relegation threatening about turn against Rochdale in late April 2014, and haven't lost away from home since Morecambe in December 2013, which spans 23 occurrences so far, all under Darrell Clarke's leadership.

A true test of character occurs not when adversity fails to strike, but precisely when it does, and this Bull believes that my beloved Rovers have passed the Hereford test so far.

# four to go, you never know

## published on Tuesday 19th April 2016

---

*Saturday 16th April - League Two*

### Bristol Rovers  2    Yeovil Town  1

Gaffney - 42', Taylor - 77'    Lita - 73'

**Rovers:** Mildenhall, Leadbitter, Lockyer, McChrystal, Brown, Montaño (Easter - 76'), Lines, O Clarke, Bodin, Taylor (Harrison - 80'), Gaffney (McBurnie - 88' [Booked]).

*Unused Substitutes:* Puddy, Parkes, Lawrence, Mansell.

Attendance: 10,264 inc 926 Non-league jokers

Referee: Paul Tierney

---

### ⊗  In recent Rovers news  ⊗

☠ In the most noteworthy news since the takeover, Lee Brown and Tom Lockyer, two of my favourite players, and part of the backbone of the the entire club (not just the team), both signed contract extensions to keep them at Rovers next season whatever division we are playing in.

☠ Cries of 'fix' went up [only joking] as DriBuild won the 1883 Sponsors Club draw to become next season's home shirt sponsors. Powersystems UK will get their catchy name on the away shirt.

---

Any Gashead user of twitter will know that this title comes from a phrase Lee Mansell started using last season, as the games ran down in our chase of Barnet and automatic promotion.

It was resurrected this season with 12 games to go, after Rovers had broke back into the top seven and spirits were high (Manse explained that he had, "crumbled to peer pressure"). The reappearance was probably a surprise as not many Rovers fans expected it would need to be dusted down and out on display again so early this season.

Given that this time of the campaign throws up fascinating games, mis-matches, relegation rucks, promotion pushes, injury crises, mental stresses, contract concerns, performance related bonuses and the occasional accusa-tion of weakened teams or players already in their flip-flops, you really do never know what is going to happen.

The one thing I think most supporters can agree on is that the top three, nor the top seven, will be fully decided until the last day of the season, and that it always seemed likely that no club was going to win all of their final five or six games, so there is no need to give up the chase after a poor result.

The season has been so tight that goal difference regularly comes into play. Our GD is uncommonly admirable this season (currently +25), and maybe, just maybe, this could be a rare season where GD could help us rather than hinder us?

Goal difference has rarely been our friend. Although everyone remembers our relegation to non-league as if it was yesterday, very few seem to mention that it was 'only' due to goal difference, and not even a particularly awful GD at that (-11, compared to Wycombe's -8). Similarly I sometimes wonder how the heck we managed to snatch relegation from the jaws of victory in 2000/01 when we had been top of the table the season previous, and went down with 51 points and a GD of only -4. Notts County also had a -4 GD and they finished eighth. In fact only a brace of teams between eight place and 24th had a better GD than us.

Returning to this season, the down side of goal difference is that there seems to be little chance of catching Oxford United's proclivity (+36) and Ports-mouth are also five better than us. Last week I was uncomfortable that Pompey were dangerously just three points behind us, with a game in hand and the aforementioned superior GD. They are however a very flaky team and their late defeat on Saturday, coupled with Accrington Stanley only drawing, has handed us a situation where we are pretty much masters of our own destiny; if we keep on winning we are unlikely to be caught.

Although in August I had a lot of enthusiasm for the opportunities this season might throw up, I am still pinching myself at just how close we have got to an automatic slot and how we have bounced back at every setback.

Looking back to March our relatively straight forward wins against Hartlepool United, Cambridge United, AFC Wimbledon and Mansfield Town now look particularly impressive. Cambridge have since held Accrington Stanley and their University rivals Oxford United, the Dons have beaten both the Janners and the Chairboys away, Mansfield have held the Cobblers and Pompey, and Hartlepool have earned 23 points in the 11 games since we humbled them 4-1. The monkey hangers are on an amazing turnaround, and could be the kingmaker's for the top three as their final four games are against Stanley (H), Oxford (A), Pompey (H), and Argyle (A).

We are riding freely with three factors which are crucial at this time of the season: a lack of injuries and suspensions; a regular ability to find the net (at least two goals in nine of the last 10 matches); and a mental and physical strength that never gives up, even when behind.

Four to go, you really never know...

# dover and dover again

## published on Saturday 23rd April 2016

*Tuesday 19th April - League Two*

### Stevenage 0    Bristol Rovers 0

**Rovers:** Mildenhall, Leadbitter (Bodin - 45'), Lockyer, McChrystal, Parkes, Brown,
Gosling (Easter - 71'), Lines, O Clarke [Booked],
Taylor, Gaffney (Harrison - 60').

*Unused Substitutes:* Puddy, Mansell. McBurnie, Montaño.

Attendance: 3,836 inc 1,327 Gasheads

Referee: Andy Madley (2nd time this season)

### ⊗   Statto Alert   ⊗

During the dreadful 2013/14 relegation season Rovers picked up 12 points against the top seven teams in the division.

This season Rovers earnt just 10. I realise there was one less team in the top seven this time (as we can't play ourselves) but it's still a rather unexpected stat.

Sometimes in life you just have to go and make your own mind up rather than listen to what other people say.

I may be an enthusiast of Neil Young, the Canadian singer-songwriter who warbles like a first round reject on The X Factor, but I almost never made it the delights of Youngsville.

I have a distinct memory of not plunging into the pool of Shakey for a very long time because I read some music critic who described his music as unlistenable, atonal and consisting mainly of feedback and industrial noises. Whilst the experimental 'album' Arc certainly was the latter, and masterpieces like 'Rust Never Sleeps' gave more than their fair share of inspiration for the 90's grunge phenomenon, Young is accessible, melodic, plays as good as the best of them and can rock like a granite quarry.

Unusually it wasn't 'After The Gold Rush' or 'Harvest' which finally turned me onto Young's unique vocal inability and capacity to craft both delightful folk songs and raging guitar wig outs, often on the same album, but his contributions to the Crosby, Stills, Nash & Young 1970 super-group classic 'Déjà Vu'.

'Ragged Glory', his distorted 1990 reunion with long time backers Crazy Horse, includes the beautiful 'Over and Over', the inspiration for the title of today's article.

Exactly a year ago I composed my feelings after our gutting draw at Dover, when holding the future in our own hands was rudely wrenched from us by a dodgy late goal in a game crying out for pace and width. It is an experience you can only truly touch and feel from being at the game, and something you ultimately need to make your own mind up about, and not be too put off by. If any of us thought that supporting your small-ish local team would be an easy ride, we might need to go and take up fishing instead.

Whilst Tuesday's insipid draw at bottom feeders Stevenage is not in the same cataclysmic category as Dover was (partly because this year we have three games left to seek atonement), it reminded me vividly of that day on the sunny South coast.

Tuesday saw almost 1,400 Gasheads invade Hertfordshire for the penultimate away game of the season, similar to the numbers who made the 2015 trip to Dover, with both on warm spring days and fans hoping to see us really cement an automatic promotion chance.

More importantly though both draws were a result of a dearth of creativity and a lack of leadership when trying to break down a resolute and impressive defence, and then getting the jitters with their decision making.

Both games offered up unexpected starting line-ups and formations. Dover saw Tom Lockyer still favoured over Daniel Leadbitter at right back, Adam Dawson was no-where to be seen, and Nathan Blissett was shoehorned into a 4-3-3 that simply failed to offer any width or penetration.

Stevenage presented us with an unforeseen return of Jake Gosling and the safety of Tom Parkes and James Clarke, thus eschewing the skills of Bodin and Monty. Macca was not in the squad at all (presumably injured?), Mansell remained unused on the bench, and there was an unanticipated switch back to a 3-5-2 that the players never got to grips with.

Whatever frailties Macca has he is an experienced leader on the pitch, as is Mansell, and they were missed when the nerves set in and our usual style of play went out the window.

Long balls, hopeful balls, percentage balls. Quite a lot of balls. If you play like that on a bobbly pitch you might as well just give up on having any tangible tactics, unless you consciously want to call that a method and take pleasure in the ball bouncing everywhere, and their lumpy centre backs winning bags of headers. This hopeful percentage game was not only dire to watch, but more importantly was never a technique that could attempt to control a vital match.

The above paragraph is actually my verbatim description of the Dover match, but you would be forgiven for thinking it was written on Wednesday morning after the late trip home from Broadhall Way.

It's only one game of course, and the season contains 46 of them, but at this business end of the year it is hard not to analyse it and to trudge away feeling like a huge opportunity had been missed, and then sense the rising anxiety that comes with your destiny no longer being in your clutches.

In the bigger picture the ragged glory of Bristol Rovers is still on the rise and judging from past bounce backs, we'll return hard and fast, and we'll still be following our men over and over again.

# sometimes it snows in April

## published on Wednesday 27th April 2016

---

### Saturday 23rd April - League Two

#### Bristol Rovers  3    Exeter City  1

Bodin - 13', Brown - 45+4',    J. Taylor - 48'
M. Taylor - 69'

**Rovers:** Mildenhall, Leadbitter, Lockyer [Booked], McChrystal, Brown [Booked], Montaño (O Clarke - 62'), Mansell. (Lawrence - 90+4'), Lines, Bodin, Taylor (Easter - 83'), Gaffney.

*Unused Substitutes:* Puddy, McBurnie, Parkes, Harrison.

Attendance:  10,254 inc 893 Grecians

Referee: Nigel Miller

---

### ⊗ Statto Alert ⊗

Only one club brought more away fans to the Mem than we took to their place, and even that wasn't really a fair fight. 553 Gasheads made it into the all-ticket affair at Luton Town on a Tuesday night, which was our fourth game in 10 days and just three days after we took 2,038 to Yeovil Town. The Hatters responded with 707 fans at the Mem, but it was a distinctly easier and more traditional Saturday crowd pleasing fixture, on the day after New Year's Day.

Note - Plymouth Argyle was the only club to sell out their away allocation (1,285 tickets) for a League match. There is therefore a possibility that extra Janners may have wanted tickets and could have eclipsed the 1,587 we took to Home Park in September.

---

At this time of the season a club's position in the table really does influence how they play. This can change game-by-game and it can be problematic for you to look into a crystal ball and expect to find the truth. As an example, we certainly caught Stevenage at a bad time, but who can prophesy how they will play in their remaining games? Their players seemed fully up for our visit and put their bodies on the line for the cause. But now they have the point they needed to make sure of League survival it's hard to predict whether they might embrace the emancipation that survival brings and play good football, or wind down and not be bothered.

Anyone can beat anyone at this time of the season, and my expectation is that this tense fortnight still holds some surprises; just like sometimes it snows in April.

Hartlepool United could have been the kingmaker's as their final four games were all against top six clubs but they made five changes for the visit of Accrington Stanley. After losing that match their manager flip-flopped and said he wouldn't stand "...for an end-of-season mentality where we're coasting and everyone wants to go on holiday"; but they still lost at Oxford United. With Pompey (H), and Plymouth Argyle (A) now almost out of the reckoning it seems too late for Darrell to ask his old club to pull their fingers out and come back down to planet earth.

Hopefully York City and Dagenham & Redbridge will be games we can comfortably win, and whilst I love sexy football I could probably handle a couple of relatively mundane wins, especially against our east London bogey team who we've only beaten once at home in four meetings since our first league fixture in 2010. It seems quite inequitable that we were relegated to non-league with 50 points when teams will only need roughly 35 to stay up this season because that duo have played like Batman and Robin having a comedy fight with the Joker. Either may still be capable of springing the odd surprise, as Plymouth found out at the weekend, but overall the ease at which both were relegated will hopefully prove the old maxim that you can dress a swine up in diamonds and pearls, but it's still a pig.

Although it's very disappointing that destiny is not in our own hands, I do quite like the simple maths that if we win both matches then we only need Accrington Stanley or Oxford United to fail to win one of their matches and, baring an unlikely goal difference swing for Stanley, we will be in the promotion news. And as they both play Wycombe Wanderers, I can hardly believe I will be thinking 'Come on you Chairboys!'.

Whatever happens we need to keep reminding ourselves that we have to enjoy being near the top of League Two for the first time ever, although I'm not sure if I'll be able to put a brave face on it if we lose in the play-offs. The last time we were consistently this high in the Football League was the infamous 1999/2000 season, and both this season and that one have proved the old adage that it can be harder to stay at the top from a decent start (e.g. Plymouth) than it is to mature and rise at the right time later in the season.

One of many marvellously positive sign of the times is that we have the second best disciplinary record in the division, with only 56 yellows, and both of the red cards given were later being rescinded on appeal. It seems unbelievable that we can (hopefully) go a whole season without a genuine red card when in 1997 we had four players sent off in just one match, when chaos and disorder reigned during a December trip to Wigan Athletic's old Springfield Park ground, before the days of under soil heating. That night, on an ice rink of a pitch, was certainly one to go in the black album labelled 'controversy', and with so few men on the pitch Rovers were forced into the rarely seen 3-1-2-1 formation!

We also have had so few injuries, which is probably a testament to the recruitment of many fit, hungry, younger players. An outfield bench versus Exeter of Ollie Clarke, Easter, Harrison, Lawrence, McBurnie and Parkes is pretty handy, and James Clarke, Jake Gosling, Rory Fallon and numerous young 'uns couldn't even get a seat at the princely table.

The building blocks are certainly there for next season, whatever League we are in, but I dearly hope that the 7th of May will include a promotion parade, and that we are partying like it's 1990 again.

Strewth, yet another secret word search, this time a very heartfelt one as I have been a big fan of the recently departed Prince since watching 'Purple Rain' in the ABC Cinema in Bath in 1984.

19 album titles were ~~heinously shoehorned in~~ delicately hidden, and the title of the article came from one of my favourite songs. Rather curiously we actually experienced snow showers on 26th & 27th April, a few days after I wrote the piece.

1st paragraph - 'For You', 'Crystal Ball / The Truth', and, 'Emancipation'

2nd para - 'Expectation' (in inimitable Prince style his album was spelt 'Xpectation')

3rd para - 'Planet Earth'

4th para - 'Lovesexy', '2010' (his Purple Highness wrote it as '20ten', natch), 'Batman', and, 'Diamonds and Pearls'

5th para - 'News' (he wrote it as 'N.E.W.S.'), and, 'Come'

6th para - 1999

7th para - 'Sign o' the Times', 'Chaos and Disorder', 'The Black Album' 'Controversy', and, '3121'

8th para - 'Prince'    9th para - 'Parade'

# an open letter to the BRFC board of directors

## published on Tuesday 3rd May 2016

*Saturday 30th April - League Two*

### York City 1    Bristol Rovers 4

McEvoy - 81'     Bodin - 19' & 71', Easter - 80',
                 Mansell - 88'

**Rovers:** Mildenhall, Leadbitter, Lockyer, McChrystal, Brown,
Montaño (Gosling - 65'), Mansell, Lines, Bodin,
Taylor (Easter - 78'), Gaffney (Harrison - 68').

*Unused Substitutes:* Puddy, McBurnie, Parkes, O Clarke.

Attendance: 4,525 inc 2,000 Gasheads

Referee: Darren Handley (2nd time this season)

### ⊗  Statto Alert  ⊗

The win at York City equalled the club record of 11 away wins in a season. The previous occurrence was whilst winning the third tier in 1989/1990.

This was Matty Taylor's 100th game for the Gas. He achieved this out of a possible maximum of 101 games since he joined Rovers in the summer of 2014; the only game he missed was the home game against FC Halifax Town in August 2014. Does this make him the fastest player to a century of appearances in a Gas shirt?

Dear Bristol Rovers (1883) Ltd Board of Directors,

Some of my fellow supporters may question the timing of this open letter, but I have been highlighting these issues since January, so after several failed attempts to influence your decision making, and no signs of discussion or action, I have to make this final public plea, which is well in time for next season, and before important supporter issues are potentially lost in a sea of promotion happiness / distraction / despair (delete as applicable - I hope it is the first one of course).

**1) Please do not label any matches next season as 'Category A' unless there is an utterly over-whelming reason or Police order to do so.**

The logic behind such price increases (an extra £4 for most tickets) was deeply flawed in League Two and many supporters cannot afford a continuation of them, especially after a season where Gasheads have also travelled away in record numbers - an average of 1,163 per League game, at an average round trip of 296 miles (from Bristol) per game, and may need to find the money for a second successive round of play-off games.

If Category A prisons are reserved for the most hardened criminals and those likely to try to escape their plight, it seems as if Category A matches at the Mem this season were some sort of punishment for loyally supporting our club in non-league last season, and now in even higher quantities this season. Our average home crowd up to, and including, Exeter City is 7,959, which is the highest since the infamous 1999/2000 season where defeat was snatched from the jaws of victory, and beyond that the highest since 1978/79. We were therefore hardly struggling for gate receipts before the imposition of these taxes.

Yet a mind bending six League games were labelled Category A by the previous regime. That was 26% of home games. Non season-ticket holders were forced to pay £20 to stand on a terrace or £23 to sit in a tent with a very poor view, and all just to watch Fourth division football in a dilapidated stadium. Season ticket holders were conveniently spared the extra cost, even though it was never mentioned as part of the 'benefits' of being able to afford the time or money to attend all home matches at the Mem. Dare I suggest they were given them 'for free' by the previous Board as otherwise they could have formed a large block of vocal disapproval against them?

A Bristol Rovers supporter who cannot get to a large majority of matches should not be penalised or looked down upon. We are all in this together and your support towards what is often disparaging labelled 'casual fans' would be appreciated. Like the Category A prisoners, all Gasheads have a life sentence they cannot escape. In reality many of these fans are not casual by choice, but have been priced out, timed out or live far away. They are irregular supporters; not casuals, part-timers, or even the dreaded expression, glory hunters. They do not 'crawl out of the woodwork' or 'appear out of no-where'.

The logic behind the entire scheme, especially in the bottom division, is rather bizarre. Most businesses would actively look forward to the few days a year when a large crowd of 'customers' is expected, and would think of innovative ways to make their experience so enjoyable that they will come back more often, rather than consciously decide to milk them dry.

If the rationale is to pay for increased Police costs, then that is also deeply unsound.

First, extra paying customers (at the usual rate), for these so-called 'bigger' games should help finance any extra costs, including via extra sales of food, drink and merchandise. Secondly, why should the supporters (both home and away) be financially penalised for who the opposition are? All football supporters want to do is to support THEIR club; they shouldn't need to take into account who the opposition are. The club should work out how best to cover any extra costs and not just lazily lump it onto the more irregular supporters.

Please scrap these nonsensical taxes on hard pressed football supporters.

Non-season ticket holders aren't cash cows. They are often historic and loyal supporters, or could be potential regulars of the future, and without future supporters a football club is nothing.

**2) Please encourage students to support us, not discourage them.**

For a huge city like Bristol, with well over 50,000 students, terminating the student category for the 2015/16 season was a PR disaster and frankly a pitiable decision. There was admittedly a new 16-21 category, but not only were the prices nowhere near as affordable as the previous student prices (£4 off most tickets, compared to £7 previously), but also not all students are under 21. Indeed in the modern era, more and more students are NOT under 21, and are proud of it, having taken years out, returned as 'mature students', are on courses lasting more than three years, or are doing post-graduate degrees, which is in itself is a massively booming market that Rovers seem to be ignoring precisely at the time Rovers are trying to build the UWE Stadium on UWE land.

Yours sincerely,

Martin Bull

## Post script

I didn't want to add the following but after receiving some flak for my THIRD attempt of the season to get anything done about prices and ticket offers, and a less than sympathetic response from the club, I felt I had to re-iterate the long time line to this campaign and add in some information that in an ideal situation would have stayed behind closed doors. The truth shall set you free apparently.

- 28th January 2016 - My article entitled 'Priced Out', was published (see pages 97 to 100), focusing on various supporter issues that were not being addressed. Brian Seymour-Smith (BR Supporters Club representative on the Board) contacted me and said he would raise the points at the next Board meeting. That board meeting was delayed and delayed. Nothing got done. No feedback received.

- 4th March 2016 - My article entitled 'Priced Out - Reloaded', was published (see pages 123 to 126), which re-iterated the previous article. I contacted Brian Seymour-Smith and he said there hadn't been a meeting yet of the new Board of Directors. Brian said he would ask for a 'quid a kid' for maybe the Cambridge United or Crawley Town match. No more feedback received. There wasn't even one 'quid a kid' offer in the entire season.

- In mid-March I wrote a new article asking the club to take a benevolent decision to scrap the Category A status for the forthcoming Exeter City and Yeovil Town games, which are not real derbies / potential Cat A games. The day it was due to be published the club announced that the last three games of the season had been made all ticket, meaning my request was already dead in the water. The article was mentioned to Steve Hamer, who asked to see it and respond directly to me. I agreed to this, but heard nothing. The ball was firmly in his court and I was not asked to contact him, or given his contact details. The Supporters Club and their representatives also never gave any information on any of these points. No contact from Brian Seymour-Smith.

- After waiting well over a month I reworked / updated the article and it was published on 3rd May 2016 (see previous pages).

- Two days later I received the following email from Steve Hamer, BRFC Chairman, via the Bristol Post -

  "I have to say that I was disappointed with the latest blog from Martin Bull that was published in your newspaper this week.

[Steve Hamer email continued] For a start, Martin opens his blog by saying that he has been highlighting the same issues since January — presumably that was to the previous Board of Directors so I and my colleagues can hardly be blamed for a lack of response as we were not even in charge at that time.

We have, as you can imagine, had a great many issues to contend with since our arrival and I am slightly disappointed at the tone of Martin's article.

His original gripe, I believe, was about reducing ticket prices because of a run of Saturday/Tuesday games and now it seems to be more about Category 'A' games and Student Prices.

In both instances the current policies were implemented by the previous Board and having inherited them there was little we could do to change things during the current season. Both of these matters are being addressed by the current Board, as you well know.

I have now mentioned, in public, the new Student App that is being introduced, that will benefit Bristol's vast student population and, in addition, it is proposed that there will be no Category 'A' games next season.

Had Martin taken the trouble to pick up the phone and speak to me, then he could have had his questions answered and would not have found the need to question, in public, the new board about previous Board's policies.

As a club we are disappointed that The Post chose to print the blog without first checking what the pricing structure was likely to be for next season.

I should be grateful if you would convey this information to Mr Bull as soon as possible and suggest that he checks his facts before going into print.

He might also like to know that we will be reviewing every aspect of our business and we are very conscious of fact that any ticket pricing structure is open to criticism and we welcome all feedback from our fans, whose loyalty and support has been crucial to our success this season."

- Without wishing to continue this issue any further I do have to re-iterate that I was clearly advised back in March that Mr. Hamer would contact me. And although officially there are no Cat A games for the 2016/17 season, early-bird prices are not being honoured on all-ticket matches [four so far], which is, in effect, a Cat A style £2 levy on such matches. This did not occur previously ☹

# the chocolate showdown

### published on friday 6th May 2016

I am (slowly) trying to visit all 92 Football League clubs. The trip to York City marked the attainment of number 71, although in a rather existential situation I was conscious that I'd be losing that club from my list of vanquishes just a week later. So had I really visited it all? 450 miles for a club already relegated endowed me with a confused 'if a tree falls down in a deserted forest does it make a sound?' moment of contemplation.

If our clubs were geographically closer this clash could be entitled the Chocolate Derby, with Rowntree's Kit Kat down the spine of the local squad, and Terry's Chocolate Orange forming a formidable barrier in goal. Fry's Chocolate Cream would feature in a strong Bristol midfield, supplying the ball to Turkish Delight out wide, the wing wizard full of eastern promise.

I was glad it wasn't us who relegated the Minstermen, as our own memories of demotion to non-league Hades are still raw and I wouldn't wish that on any fans, except maybe some of those south of the river. York of course have been there before (relegated in 2004 to end 75 years of League membership, and bouncing back eight seasons later) but that will hardly sweeten the bitter pill for their loyal fans.

As for us, the end of this season feels like Groundhog Day, as for the third year in a row we go into the final game hoping to get the right result for ourselves and / or hoping other results go our way. Both previous editions ended in tears, so I am protecting my heart with logic and envisaging that Saturday will most probably not end the way we want it to, even though we are a rampant team now, full of goals (Stevenage was the only time we haven't scored since February).

Waiting for an in-form rival to slip up at home, whilst being mindful to do the business yourself, is a desolate existence, even if it is heartening to still have the prospect of automatic promotion.

I vividly remember last April as we tried to grasp feathers floating in the wind and scoured the stats to rationalize the optimism that Gateshead could give Barnet a really tough time. The reality was that Barnet were an exceptional side and Gateshead weren't, and with home advantage and a Heed side decimated by injuries, we were clutching at emotional straws.

I was there at Dover when we witnessed the control of our future slip out of our hands, just as I was there at Stevenage to see it come to pass again. I was also on the terrace against Alfreton Town when we dreamt that Jake Gosling's early strike would put some pressure on Barnet. Alas Mauro Vilhete scored for the Bees just a handful of minutes later, and never before had a 7-0 win in front of a packed house been so deflating. Maybe it is me who should stay away?

If Oxford United and Accrington Stanley both win on Saturday they will have deserved promotion as they are both excellent teams, with capable managers. 'The club that wouldn't die' have achieved the amazing on a tiny budget, and the U's have kept their nerve (unlike Plymouth Argyle) and ridden an ominous injury crisis.

Although I am certainly not the sort of person who complains about so-called little clubs progressing up the football ladder, whilst older or 'bigger' ones flounder (usually deservedly so due to mismanagement and arrogance), I have to admit Saturday will be tinged with disappointment if Accrington Stanley go up at the direct expense of us.

Whilst I have fond memories of the Accrington area from a recent period of living 'up north' (or more accurately the marvellous graffiti den at the nearby derelict Huncoat power station), and in some ways would love to see their prudent management rewarded, I genuinely think they will struggle if they gain their first ever season in League One whereas a back-to-back promotion for us could be something that really pushes and encourages our team and our new owners onto higher endeavours.

Star players Josh Windass (who came back from injury just in time to propel their promotion charge) and Matt Crooks (who was chosen for the PFA League Two Team of the Year) have already signed pre-contracts with Glasgow Rangers and will leave Lancashire at the end of the season, and although Billy Kee has slightly strangely done the opposite by accepted a new contract in the full knowledge of the above, I think Stanley will really miss that duo and with crowds and income unlikely to increase much, they will struggle.

Like a chocolate taster at Somerdale I'm almost sick with the twists and turns these three seasons have thrown up. Saturday can't come soon enough, as my sheltered heart can finally be allowed out for a little breathing space.

# karma chameleon
### published on Tuesday 10th May 2016

---

*Saturday 7th May - League Two*

**Bristol Rovers  2    Dagenham & Redbridge  1**

Bodin - 15', Brown - 90+2'    Cash - 12'

**Rovers:** Mildenhall, Leadbitter, Lockyer, McChrystal, Brown [Booked], Montaño (Gosling - 55'), Mansell (Easter - 80'), Lines, Bodin, Taylor, Gaffney (Harrison - 66').

*Unused Substitutes:* Puddy, McBurnie, Parkes, O Clarke.

Attendance: 11,130 inc 291 stoic & loyal Daggers (they had already been relegated)

Referee: Stuart Attwell

---

⊗ **Statto Alert** ⊗

☠ This was the first Rovers promotion sealed in Bristol since April 1953.

☠ Lee Brown's incredible late goal also gave us a record breaking eight double wins during the season. The previous record of seven doubles was achieved in 1952/53, 1963/64, 1989/90 & 1993/94.

☠ Rovers were the only team in League Two to never draw two matches in a row, and were also the only team with a 100% Half Time to Full Time win record. In the 11 matches where Rovers were leading at Half Time, we carried on to win all of them at Full Time.

---

I still genuinely can't quite believe that Saturday happened. Although I believed we could win, and that there was obviously some chance of Oxford United or Accrington Stanley failing to win, I never expected it to be quite so dramatic.

As the 80th minute was approaching the situation was getting forlorn so I took my mind off the tension by formulating a headline for this weeks article; 'We all live on a yellow substitution', a hideous mash-up of a classic Beatles song. My reasoning was that the surprise Daggers substitution at half-time seemed to have worked well; shoring up their left back area which was getting over-run in the first half by Billy Bodin and Daniel Leadbitter. Bodin looked to be the only man on the pitch with the composure to get a winner for us, yet he was finding space much tougher to locate after their reshuffle.

Nervous pressure was getting the better of several players on the pitch with Rory Gaffney, Matty Taylor and Lee Mansell in particular failing to take relatively easy chances to bang in a goal or six. I'm certainly not blaming them; I imagine very few League Two players have been in that sort of atmosphere and weighty situation before, and even if they had it is no guarantee that butterflies can't still flutter in your tummy.

By now I felt it wasn't going to happen for us, although that was partly just my head trying to protect my fragile heart, weakened by years of failure, near misses and an inferiority complex that hung like a shadow over our club.

But if there is just one thing us Rovers fans should have learnt this season (and to some extent last season) it is that we should NEVER give up, because our team doesn't.

Of course the late charge doesn't always come off, but this set of players are fit and determined and certainly do try until the final seconds, and the stats back it up; Rovers rescued 20 points from losing positions this season, and scored 54 second half goals (the joint highest in League Two), of which 20 came in the last 10 minutes (the second highest).

35 shots on goal, about half of which were on target.

17 corners.

Several golden chances.

Numerous slaps on the woodwork.

But nothing would creep in, and all this against the back drop of an inspired goal keeping performance and an opposition who, like Stevenage just a few weeks ago, were tiger-ish in defence of their dignity, and also tidy up top. The Daggers certainly came with a sense of freedom of expression and did not sit back or waste time.

The turning point came in the 82nd minute when Tom Lockyer made a vital goal line clearance. It was crucial, even if occurred slightly in slow-mo. My belief returned. A little. Maybe karma could be changing its colour after all? Maybe our final day relegation at the Mem on goal difference, after a shock goal in off a post in front of the Blackthorn faithful, really could be turned on its head?

If there is a karma billionaire out there his name isn't actually Wael Al Kadi, but Lee Brown. The man who has the most Gas appearances of the current squad, the man who missed out on that Mansfield match at the last minute but stayed with us because he felt it was the right thing to do, the man who is awaiting the arrival of his second golden child, and most importantly the man who played every second of all 50 games of this season.

A remarkable statistic for a remarkably fit and reliable man.

It could hardly have been more fitting that fate chose Browner to bash in the winning goal in the 4,500th minute of his season. The only more apt scorer could have been if the ball had been mysteriously sucked into the net by the spirit of those Rovers loyalists who've sadly left us in recent times, including Ben Hiscox, Barrie Meyer, Ray Spearing, and Paul Withey.

As much as I feel sorry for Accrington fans that one of three exceptional teams had to miss out, at least they can sleep soundly in the knowledge that none of our recent opponents gave less than 100%. The end to this season re-iterated why all fans ought to have hope and should keep on following their team however depressing it gets because you never quite know what is going to happen when a ball is on a patch of grass and 22 players are kicking the... cough... out of it.

Well, I'm back to where I started supporting Rovers, in the third tier, and that feels good.

Karma may come and go but it will get there in the end.

# heaven must be missing an angelo

**published on Thursday 19th May 2016**

**⊗ Statto Alert ⊗**

☠ The 36 away goals that Rovers scored was the third highest in our history, beaten only by the 37 in 1952/53 and 39 in 1963/64.

☠ Rovers finished the season on a winning streak of nine consecutive home League games. The club record of 10, set in 1935, was equalled at the first home game of the 2016/17 season, but couldn't be bettered.

In April Darrell Clarke once again made it public that all out of contract senior players would get a new offer at the end of the season... if the small matter of promotion was secured. This is a motivational ploy that seems to have worked well, and has also helped keep a successful squad together.

I for one was ecstatic when Tom Lockyer and Lee Brown, truly players who are first on the team sheet, and have many years left in them, signed new contracts even before the end of the season, and we have already heard that Steve Mildenhall has signed a new one year deal.

These guaranteed offers may not be exactly what the player and their agent may wish for though, and last season a few choose to find their fortune elsewhere, with Andy Monkhouse preferring Grimsby Town, Angelo Balanta upping sticks for a mammoth move up North to Carlisle United, and Neal Trotman giving up a chance to train with the squad to help get his fitness back after injury, and have some prospect of finding a deal elsewhere (he never did...).

Back in January on Geoff Twentyman's first episode of his new weekly BBC Radio Bristol 'Having a Gas' programme, there was a telling moment when Lee Mansell humbly described Balanta's penalty in the 2015 Promotion Play-off Final at Wembley as the pressure penalty rather than his.

It's a year since that gut wrenching day, and looking back he has a point.

After three spot-kicks each we were 3-2 up as Jon-Paul Pitman had just sent his effort to join the International Space Station. If Angelo's pen went in we would be 4-2 up and piling mental pressure on Craig Clay, his fishy counterpart.

Mansell was modest enough to conclude that although us fans might see his pen as the critical one, and treat him as a hero, he felt he had little to lose; if he scored he had won promotion for us, but if he failed the shoot-out continued and the Mariners would still need to net their fifth just to get back to level pegging and ensure more tension followed.

Andy Monkhouse was sixth in our queue, and Tom Lockyer was just behind him. Both were apparently dreading taking a penalty, which hardly puts faith in them to have converted if it came to them. Even worse was that one of our two strikers on the pitch wasn't in the line yet and was lower on the list than a 20 year old makeshift right-back who has only scored two career goals in almost 150 appearances, and at the time was being regularly berated for his wayward passing.

At this point I must make a terrible confession. It is dreadful not in its magnitude (I didn't murder anyone or torture ants with a magnifying glass as a kid) but grave because I am admitting I had so little faith in a Rovers player that I didn't actually want him to volunteer to take a penalty anyway. Judging from the fact that striker Nathan Blissett wasn't even on the list of our first seven takers, I'd suggest he also didn't want to take one and my lack of faith was quite well founded.

Bearing in mind that Ellis Harrison had already been subbed off and Jermaine Easter was out injured, it does make you wonder what terrible conclusion could have transpired if Jon-Paul Pitman hadn't missed his one.

So, just for that one fleeting moment alone Angelo Balanta deserves a special little place in Rovers folklore, perhaps alongside Sammy Igoe for his keystone cops goal to settle the 2007 promotion play-off, and Andy Rammell for his Rambo heroics to avoid the drop in 2003.

Despite being offered a new deal with Rovers (after only three starts and 15 sub appearances), Angelo surprisingly moved 275 miles to Scotland (well, it might as well be...) where he managed the grand total of four League starts, three sub appearances, and a trio of Cup starts. He matched his Rovers goal record with a solitary goal, in the only League game the Cumbrians won with him on the grass.

His final appearance of the season was in mid-November against, yes, you guessed it, us. Given that he hadn't played football since September this unlikely homecoming seemed to be an object lesson in psychology from the eminent Professor K Curle, hopeful that a tasty game against his old team might wake him from his slumber.

The object lesson was an abject failure, as Rovers cruised in third gear to an opportune 2-0 win, our first home League triumph since August, although as both goals came after Angelo had been replaced, maybe he could claim that defeat was nothing to do with him?

As if signalling an end to Rovers' golden era, that day also saw the final appearance of Mr. Blissett in a blue and white quartered shirt, a two minute cameo where the habitually errant BBC live text update service was given a chance to capture his final fleeting moments for posterity; "A Nathan Blissett pass catches Nathan Blissett offside".

And so it came to pass.

It demonstrates the quality and popularity of our current squad that few fans would be content to see more than one or two turn down their new contract offers this time around.

Angelo was released by Carlisle last week, presumably to take his place in Rovers heaven.

# pick of the promotion pops

### this was originally published as five parts between
### Tuesday 31st May and Monday 20th June 2016.
### I have presented them here all together, as it flows better.

Greetings pop pickers and welcome to this special edition of Pick of the Pops, this time featuring the year 2015/16, focusing on 10 golden themes or moments in an unprecedented second promotion in two seasons for BRFC.

*Note - this BRFC definitely isn't (Tony) Blackburn Rovers, and the picked pops aren't in any precise order of magnitude.*

So, join me over the next few weeks to witness how Darrell Clarke and his lads overturned a miserable recent history of relegations with 50 points, and goal difference going against us, with an added time goal that caused chaos at the Mem and somehow appeased the Gods of Goal Difference as well.

Are Gasheads still in wonderland? Not 'arf.

## number 10 - the strongest benches we've seen for many years

After enduring only five spaces on a Conference bench, a season back in the Football League gave us seven spots to fill, and with a hungry squad and a distinct lack of injuries or suspensions, we often saw the strongest benches we've seen for many years, maybe even since the days around the dawn of the new Millennium when the likes of Nathan Ellington, Bobby Zamora, Mark Walters, and Clinton Ellis graced the wood.

This was particularly telling towards the end of the season, when a few new faces had arrived, and no-one had left. The outfield bench against Exeter City (a match that could have been a real banana skin) was Ollie Clarke, Jermaine Easter, Ellis Harrison, Liam Lawrence, Ollie McBurnie and Tom Parkes. In anyone's language that offered a great mix of experienced and up and coming players. James Clarke, Jake Gosling, Rory Fallon and numerous young 'uns couldn't even get a seat at the table.

Even more importantly it often gave the flexibility DC needed to make decisive changes, often including a formation change. The spirit of Bob Bloomer, the archetypal utility man, clearly lived on in the suppleness of the 2015/16 squad, and unlike a vision of Adam Virgo marauding up and down the left wing like Roberto Carlos in his pomp (...not!), they did actually play in their strongest position the majority of the time.

## number 9 - goals galore

You don't need a Ph.D. in Football Genius to know that if you have goals in your side you'll always hold the possibility of success in your hands. Even Kevin Keegan's Newcastle United stood a chance for most games despite not knowing that the word defend was in the dictionary. Ok, so you might occasionally let in four (or in our case three to Carlisle United) but more often than not you'll have a win under your belt if you played your cards right.

Although the striker spotlight naturally fell on 27 goal man Matty Taylor, the little magician would be humble enough to admit that the service he and others got last season was impeccable at times, with Chris Lines supplying nine assists, plus six each from Lee Brown and Daniel Leadbitter on the flanks. Tellingly 10 of those 21 assists went the way of Taylor himself.

Although Rovers held firm to the strange statistic of only one defender scoring all season (Lee Brown with six), and only a Wiltshire handful of goals from central midfield (Lee Mansell, Ollie Clarke and The Beard had a brace each), up-top and out wide is always the heart of the matter for any team; the rest is a bonus. Billy Bodin was a sensation with 13 goals, Rory Gaffney came on loan, stayed, and contributed eight strikes, Ellis Harrison had a rather quiet season but still put away seven vital wallops, all away from home and three of them late penalties, and Jermaine Easter also bagged seven.

With goal scoring like that, ducks from James Clarke (38 matches), Jake Gosling (18), Daniel Leadbitter (33), Chris Lines (33), Tom Lockyer (43), Mark McChrystal (21), and Tom Parkes (31) could be forgiven, even if they were given an astonishing 217 appearances between them to try to hit a barn door with a banjo.

## number 8 - a complete turnaround in home form

After failing to score in four of our first six home League games, and gaining just four points, Rovers then scored in all of the next 17 at the Mem, with a W14 D1 L2 record, and finished with the second best home record in League Two.

Rovers were unbeaten at home after late November and finished the season on a streak of nine consecutive wins, which means the team still have a chance to equal our longest ever run (10 on the trot in 1935) at the opening home game of the League One season.

## number 7 - return of the Mild

No, this is not an oblique reference to a cleaning product, a weak beer, or even Mark Morrison's signature hit, but the re-integration of Steve Mildenhall as first choice keeper, and ditching the uncomfortable reliance on loanee's from other clubs.

After some weak performances during the run-in to the end of the Conference season Mildy was replaced as first choice keeper by Will Puddy and didn't feature again until his dramatic 119th minute Wembley entrance to face the penalty shoot-out that catapulted Rovers back to the Football League. His shot-stopping had never been under question, but his command of the box and distribution of the ball was.

As August came upon us Puddy was on the treatment table and Mildy was given a 'final' chance to stake his claim to be number one keeper again. But after only the first two games of the season, DC decided to draw on the loan market instead, with Aaron Chapman from Chesterfield between the sticks for five games, and Lee Nicholls from Wigan Athletic getting 18 games under his young belt; indeed, Nicholls was still in pre-school when Mildenhall made his League debut in 1997.

Despite Mildenhall being the keeper on the bench throughout Nicholls' mediocre loan spell, Will Puddy was rushed back to take his place between the posts for the first game after his departure, a trip to east London in mid-December. In the 50th minute Puddy was struck by a recurrence of his groin problem and Mildy was offered an early Chrimbo present; a huge Yuletide redemption log. Co-incidentally at the final whistle of the velvety 3-0 win Rovers found themselves in the play-offs for the first moment of the season, replacing, yes, Mansfield Town. Amiable karma was alive and kicking again.

Stuck with Mildenhall as the only fit keeper the atmosphere seemed to be tense for a while, as questions were left dangling in the air. Would DC plump for another loanee? Had any bridges been burnt on either side? Could humble pie be on the lunch menu? But most crucially for us fans - was Mildy up to the job?

Thankfully all the questions were answered just as we desired. Mildy slowly showed that he had improved his game whilst on the sidelines, and reports filtered out that he had been a model professional during his bench warming days; still passionate and resolute about his job, and still encouraging to the very young 'uns who were usurping him (well, they do say it is a barmy little club they all belong to...).

Mildy played for the rest of the season, grew in confidence as his form returned and made some spectacular saves which helped earn some crucial points. But more importantly, he and others like Ellis Harrison and Jake Gosling showed that the special spirit in the squad wasn't confined just to the ones getting regular games, but also to those at the periphery, those loaned out, or in Mildy's case, even those publicly deemed surplus to requirements.

## number 6 - it could be worse, we could be Yeovil Town

Only six loan players were used all season, and none of them were heavily relied upon. I see this as a confident shift in strategy because numerous loanee's can be the sign of an incomplete, transient or problematic squad, or even worse, having a defective manager at the helm. Loanee's will rarely buy you longer-term success and stability.

Whilst Lee Nicholls and fellow keeper Aaron Chapman did contribute a valuable 23 appearances between them they weren't actually covering for injury as Steve Mildenhall was fit and on the bench for all bar one of their appearances. Their recruitment was calculated rather than compulsory.

And whilst Rory Gaffney certainly had a significant impact on the team whilst on loan from Cambridge United, even he was mainly a 'shake up' signing at first, as Jermaine Easter and Ellis Harrison warmed the bench for most of his seven match loan period.

Paris Cowan-Hall made two starts, one sub appearance, and remained on the bench twice, Ollie McBurnie received game time from the bench for his first five games, but then sat unused for his final four, and the forgotten hero of promotion, Jeffrey Monakana, made three appearances off the bench at the very start of the season, and took the weight off his feet for a further trio of games. He currently works in a Subway. As a busker. Maybe. Or holds the bizarre squad number 77 for FC Voluntari (est. 2010) in Romania. One of the above is actually true.

It seems clear that our squad was far stronger in League Two and that DC now had the time, experience and maybe budget to assemble a far more complete team. Compare this to the non-league season hotchpotch of Dave Martin, Adam Cunnington, Alex Wall, Bradley Goldberg, Fabian Spiess, Lyle Della-Verde, Josh Wakefield, Adam Dawson and Chris Lines, with an improbable 58 starts, and 24 sub appearances between them.

Only Mr. Lines currently plays in League football. I rest my case your Honour.

## number 5 - injuries, suspensions and beast mood

To gain promotion you need the almost perfect season to transpire, where everything from finances to fitness, and teamwork to tactics, slots neatly into place.

A little dash of good fortune can help as well, and although I do believe that recruitment of younger and / or fitter players without a bad injury record can help, and a dynamic fitness and lifestyle ethos can make a difference, it would be unfair to suggest, for example, that all of the numerous **injuries** Rovers endured in the relegation season were avoidable, or that giving a fresh chance to Billy Bodin after a year of virtually no football following an Anterior Cruciate Ligament (ACL) injury, was a masterstroke that could never have possibly gone pear shaped.

The Rovers staff and players can however certainly take some considerable credit for never having an injury crisis, for boasting fitness levels never seen before at the club (even when training at an Army camp in the village of my birth) and for never relying on a plethora of loan players (only 23 different players started games for the Pirates).

Rovers went the whole season without any hugely debilitating injuries, and for a relatively small and tight knit squad whose well drilled whole was more than the sum of its parts that had a substantial positive effect. Whilst it became routine for rival managers to whinge about their injuries, and to be fair Plymouth Argyle and Oxford United truly did suffer towards the end of the season, for us only Will Puddy and Stuart Sinclair were injured for any sizeable period of time.

Although I was a fan of Will Puddy in the Conference I was never sure he was a real solution to a problem position, and would have happily witnessed one top-notch keeper replace both Puddy and Mildenhall in the summer of 2015, so his absence for half of this season was hardly an injury to be too despondent about.

As much as I love The Beard, his whole-hearted style of play puts his tiny frame under such strain it is no surprise it seems to snap under the pressure; recollect his leap at Gateshead on the final day of February 2015, and his subsequent fall back to earth from the stratosphere in a crumpled heap. This season was almost a carbon copy, starting all bar one of the opening 35 League and cup games, and only leaving the pitch early at two of those games, but then missing all of the final 15 games through injury.

Revisionist historians are already negating his positive influence to the team, suggesting we hit our best form with him out injured and that he won't be able to handle the step up to League One. These are probably the same detractors who said he wouldn't make an impact in League Two football, after making that breakthrough at the ripe age of 26. Although it was certainly true that it was hard to know quite how to fit him into a midfield that had so many contradictory options, with wildly differing skill sets, and which regularly faced changes in formation not just between games but also during the game, it is entirely unfair to lay these wider strategic problems on his golden teaselled locks.

In a perfect world I think the Beard would always deserve his place in a Rovers midfield, the difficult part is getting the team balance right. Every midfield can benefit from a Sinclair type terrier, and he has a quicker turn of pace and a better eye for a pass than many critics give him credit for.

Intriguingly the player who was statistically missed the most was Mark McChrystal who was injured for the opening eight games and an unused sub for the next two. Six of those games ended in defeat; in fact Macca only featured in three of the 13 League defeats, whilst in contrast he played in 16 wins and three draws.

**Discipline** is something that can be controlled more clearly than injuries and more often than not effective discipline comes from the top. DC and his staff therefore deserve recognition for the team finishing with the second best disciplinary record in the division, with only 57 yellow cards, and both red cards that were given out were rescinded on appeal. Only Exeter City were better, with 53 yellows and no reds of any description or inaccuracy. This record also meant that Rovers did not lose any player to any suspension for the whole season; quite an achievement, and certainly gave us a slight advantage over our competitors, in a league where ultimately just four goals in eight long months made the difference between promotion and failure.

It was no surprise that Mansfield Town were the worst disciplined with 85 yellows, three double yellows and three straight reds. Our old fair play friends Notts County were next in line; obviously not a lot changes in the east Midlands.

One of the most comical moments of the season came when AFC Wimbledon visited the Mem in early March. The phoenix club exhibited impressive pace, power and passing, especially upfront, and were without an away loss since October. But Rovers sliced through them and with 10 minutes left were 3-1 up. The impressive Lyle Taylor was substituted, with Adebayo 'The Beast' Akinfenwa being winched on as a last roll of the not-so fluffy dice.

Within minutes he was constantly fouling and seemed to think that because he is famed as 'the strongest idiot' on the FIFA Football video game series he was somehow authorised to push opposing players away from him at arms length, presumably so that he could get his way (as usual, it's always about him...) and score a goal unimpeded.

When the referee gave a free kick against him he threw his toys out of the pram to such a degree that his throbbing head and windmilling arms were temporarily the only things on earth that could be spotted from Outer Space. A red card was brandished and he huffed and puffed before finally trudging off, remonstrating with thin air as if on a powerful LSD trip.

If there are two men in the world who could unquestionably start a fight in an empty room, their names are Adebayo Akinfenwa and Donald Trump. There was a third but Ronald Reagan is dead.

And the point is? Well, for all the weaknesses and faults of our players, I can't see any of them acting like that (ok... well, I have just thought of one maybe...), and I'm sure DC wouldn't stand for it if one of them ever did. We have no prima donnas, no crazy hatchet men, and no media whores, and long may that continue. I can take passion, and the odd heat of the moment crime, but unbridled arrogance I can live without.

## number 4 - a debt of gratitude to the land of leeks, male choirs and Ivor the Engine

Although I am loathed to single out individual players, I am about to do just that.

After the Wembley nail-biter in 2015 I wrote a series of five articles about the relatively unsung heroes of promotion out of non-league. The more 'obvious' heroes, such as Matty Taylor and Lee Mansell, weren't allowed to be featured. To some degree I am doing the same here, as although any 27 goal striker is automatically a unique piece in a promotion puzzle, our climb actually benefited more from two young Welsh players whose outstanding seasons went well beyond what most pundits expected of them.

I feel no dishonour when recalling that I did not enjoy watching **Tom Lockyer** playing at right back for most of the Conference season, ahead of Daniel Leadbitter. I stand by that sentiment. It was often unduly cautious, and I don't like players out of position on anything more than an occasional basis. Although I could appreciate Tom's effort in each and every game, and in general his remarkable appearance stats for one so young, playing acutely out of position meant I could not thoroughly perceive the player that was inside him, longing to escape the imposed shackles.

This season I certainly could.

What a centre back this lad is, and how enjoyable it is to watch him there. Tom may not be the biggest, the strongest, or even the fastest, but put together his broad attributes, and add into the mix a calmness that belies his age, a growing physical strength and rapidly improving ball skills, and you have a class act sitting on your own doorstep.

I am confident that he will be another in a long line of Rovers' centre backs who prove themselves to be so good, yet so young, that they got the opportunity of almost a decade at the top of the football tree. This is not just hyperbole. I truly believe that Tom is the most prized asset of our squad and is in the Larry Lloyd, Gary Mabbutt and Steve Yates category.

I may never completely understand how **Billy Bodin** didn't get more League games this season (25 starts + 11 sub appearances), but I'm sure that after his recent run in a successful team he was very high up the list of players that really justified being retained and paid more.

Dismissed as a luxury player by some, and having missed virtually the whole of last season first to a Anterior Cruciate Ligament (ACL) injury and later to a lack of game time when on a short-term contract at Northampton Town, he was almost in danger of being a forgotten newbie after a stop-start beginning at Rovers.

But for me, the first time I saw those beautiful feet in action I swooned like I haven't swooned since Muzzy Carayol danced his way down wings and scored spectacular goals out of the blue. Anyone with slaloming skills like Billy (crucial goals at York City and in the promotion decider on the final day of the season were both George Best-esque) deserves to be regularly seen by paying supporters because it is simply so rare, and so unexpected, in the fourth tier.

Naturally such players are frustrating at times, and are hounded by the moans and groans of those fans who prefer their wide-men of the more staid variety, but to me they are essential for any team who wish to create chances, to score goals, and to dare to entertain. After all, football is an entertainment pursuit; a leisure time escape from the grumbles of our own rotten lives. And yet we paid to witness the sight of Robbie Ryan, Mark Wright and Andy Bond down the flanks, all of whom came complete with an open hotline to the Samaritans.

Billy reminds me of the mercurial Jeff Hughes and my Gerry Francis-era hero, David Mehew, both players with a real eye for a goal, and liable to unexpectedly pop up anywhere on the pitch (sometimes in completely the wrong place!). This element of surprise is very effective; if the player doesn't comprehend what position he's playing, what chance do the opposition have?

Although I would not want to see too many of the squad leave in the next few weeks, I am quietly calm at the moment. The decisive business has already been done, with Bodin, Brown, Leadbitter and Lockyer already settled. Add in James Clarke, Rory Gaffney, Lee Mansell, Steve Mildenhall and Stuart Sinclair and the squad is steadily taking shape.*

*By the time the article was published Mark McChrystal and Ellis Harrison had both signed new deals and our first new signing (Peter Hartley) had also occurred. Within two days Byron Moore had arrived as well and Cristian Montaño signed his new deal. So five players in three days rather changed the equation above! The point I was trying to make though was that I see Bodin, Brown, Leadbitter and Lockyer as the key contracts to tie-up (plus Matty Taylor of course). The rest are bonuses and more easily replaceable.*

## number 3 - a Spring return to decent away form

When our home form was dreadful (seven points from our first nine games), our away form kept our head above water, with 19 points from our first nine games. By New Year's Day Rovers had gained 24 away points from 12 matches.

A winter depression saw our away form disintegrate (four losses in five, mainly to play-off rivals) and even the turn around in home form couldn't keep us from temporarily dropping as low as tenth place.

But after the placid loss in the quaint village of West Wycombe results perked up at a pivotal time of the year, with 11 points from our final six away games, including the following valiant rescue mission...

## number 2 - one, two, buckle my shoe

Whilst it is impossible to single out one specific point as **the** one that ultimately pulled us level on points with Accrington Stanley, just like you can't pick out just a couple of the goals that made our goal difference superior, the 2-2 draw at Northampton Town in April was possibly the most important salvaged point of the season given: (a) the circumstances - two down with 15 minutes left; (b) the opposition - unbeaten since Christmas and top since 23rd January; and, (c) the occasion, as the Cobblers had to win to guarantee promotion in front of their own fans, and although they gained promotion anyway, thanks to Plymouth Argyle losing to a typically blustering 88th minute 'Beast' goal, they were not to know that was going to happen.

Whilst the aftermath of the final whistle was bitter sweet because we lost our space in the automatic promotion slots (again! this time to Stanley, who won at Luton Town), in the long run that point was crucial.

## at number 1, the top of the promotion pops, we have -

### wait for it...

### yes, it's coming...

### it really is... it's just around the corner...

### honestly, trust me... I can see it coming over the hill...

### oops, it might have to go on the next page now...

## but first a quick reminder on the run-down so far...

At Number 10 we had the strongest benches we've seen for many years,

At Number 9 we witnessed goals galore,

At Number 8 we experienced a complete turnaround in home form,

At Number 7 we pondered the return of the Mild and the attitude of other fringe players,

At Number 6 we celebrated not touching the Yeovil Town syndrome with a barge pole, a.k.a. when half your squad belong to someone else,

At Number 5 we held an in-depth inquiry into the lack of injuries, suspensions, and, thankfully, any beast moods on the pitch,

At Number 4 we identified a debt of gratitude to the land of leeks, male choirs and Ivor the Engine,

At Number 3 we revealed a Spring return to decent away form,

At Number 2 we had the cryptic title of one, two, buckle my shoe, and

### at number 1, the top of the promotion pops, we have -

# rescuing 20 points from losing positions

If a wag had made a T-shirt in the summer of 2014 boldly exclaiming 'Bristol Rovers - Snatching defeat from the jaws of victory since 1883' we could hardly have condemned his ridicule too much.

The truth hurts. But the truth will also set you free.

By that same Autumn Rovers were a different beast and began to show a resilience and a never say die attitude that had previously gone walkabout for what seemed like an eternity.

The tenacity shown in front of the live TV cameras against Gateshead in December 2014 (winning after twice being behind, and all only six days after the mortifying FA Trophy defeat to Bath City); the perseverance exhibited at Halifax Town in March 2015 (two down with seven minutes left); and, the fortitude displayed at Wembley (battered by the Mariners from the first whistle and clearly showing nerves), all pursued the Pirates into League Two.

Rovers came back six times from a goal down to win, versus Cambridge United (Away), York City (Home), Oxford United (A), Morecambe (H), Newport County (A), and finally the mother of them all, Dagenham & Redbridge (H). Two crucial away points were also filched at the death, at Plymouth Argyle and the Cobblers.

Rovers were now experts at grasping victory from the jaws of defeat; scoring a staggering 54 second half goals, including 20 goals in the last 10 minutes.

Those 20 rescued points are not just a nice figure for geeks to stand back and admire though. The points were gained not by luck but by judgement. By hard work. By an unswerving attention to detail.

The detail of carefully choosing the right players for the squad, and then choosing the right players for the right match. The detail of mentally conditioning players to work as a team, and to be winners at whatever they do. The detail of demanding peak fitness and giving them the tools to achieve it. The detail of creating a tight knit, competitive, yet friendly and relaxed, dressing room.

In March the Bristol Post's excellent chief sports writer Steve Cotton recalled a text he had from Chris Giles, Darrell Clarke's former skipper at Salisbury, who recollected how DC 'bonds lads like I've never known', and singled out his 'genius banter'.

A UEFA Pro License is needed to manage at the top level and it can be studied for and achieved by anyone with a reasonable intellect and football knowledge (Mark McGhee got his way back in 2003), but there is no course available for genius banter, nor any certificate that can be proudly displayed on a corpulent Premier League office wall.

In April I mentioned Hereford FC's charming motto; 'Our greatest glory lies not in never having fallen, but in rising when we fall'. Gasheads can now truly understand that motto because we have lived it and emerged out of the other side of a dark tunnel as a 'proper' club once again.

All hail the new Bristol Rovers, under the leadership of Darrell Clarke.

Not 'arf.

# Epilogue

Well, what a season.

I'm still metaphorically gasping for air. I'd never been at a League match where Rovers have gained promotion and after suffering at the Mem for the last game of the regular season in the previous two years, this one made a vastly refreshing change. I doubt I will ever see another afternoon quite like it, and after 27 years as a Gashead I thought I'd lived through most scenarios.

Promotion out of League Two took us 2,115 days first time around; this time it was merely 274 days, so for every one of those days a copy of this book has been printed. Which day is your day? [see the Introduction if you haven't already clocked it]

Gone was the inferiority complex, gone was the glass half-full syndrome - 'nothing good happens to Rovers' - and gone were the Paul Simon lyrics in my head - "hello darkness my old friend, I've come to talk with you again".

Instead of the sound of silence we were back on speaking terms with karma, our omnipresent bedfellow. She had previously punished our club for its bloated arrogance, but was now permitting it to flourish after bouts of self - flagellation and restoring the heart of gold back into the core of the club.

All the supporters club volunteers, all the staff who went beyond the call of duty, all the fans who turned up week after week to watch the spineless dross we were served up, and even those who came less but still stood up and labelled themselves Gasheads and Pirates; all were rewarded for their loyalty in the presence of intense provocation.

If there is one thing us Rovers fans have learnt since DC took over it is that we should NEVER give up, because our team doesn't now.

I'm back to where I started supporting Rovers, in the third tier, and like a kind word from a caring person, that feels good. Very good.

I hope you enjoyed the book. Please send any comments / feedback to me at hello@awaythegas.org.uk and I hope you'll find time to contribute to the forthcoming 'Twerton Delight' book (see page 138 for details).

### Take care & UTG!    Martin

# ACTIVITY TIME
## MAKE YOUR OWN SOUNDTRACK TO THIS BOOK

You may have noticed that I'm a big music fan. I adore music popping into my head as I write and using it as inspiration for articles, as a connection, or even as just a feeling (yes, that is a Bad Manners reference...see, I just can't stop it).

So, if you share my taste in music (Note - I don't necessarily love all the inspirations, especially, cough, the 80's kiddie pop - I was young and naive! Honest guv), find the tracks below, print out the CD cover, and create your own soundtrack to this book.

---

### DOUBLE DARRELL - The Soundtrack to Your Rovers Life

1. Dave & Ansell Collins - Double Barrel [Title of the book]
2. Lead Belly - Goodnight Irene [Every Article]
3. Bob Dylan - Blowin' in the Wind [Article 1]
4. The Hollies - He Ain't Heavy, He's my Brother [Article 7]
5. De La Soul - The Magic Number [Article 12]
6. Pulp - Do you Remember the First Time? [Article 13]
7. Cat Stevens - Tea for the Tillerman [Article 20]
8. David Bowie - Let's Dance [Article 23]
9. Wham! Wham! & more Wham! [Article 25]
10. Elvis Costello - I Don't Want to go to Chelsea [Article 26]
11. Timbuk3 - The Future's so Bright, I Gotta Wear Shades [Article 27]
12. R.E.M. - Automatic for the People [Article 31]
13. The Stranglers - Golden Brown [Article 32]
14. Neil Young - Over and Over Again [Article 38]
15. Any song from the late and genuinely great Prince [Article 39]
16. Culture Club - Karma Chameleon [Article 41]
17. Tavares - Heaven Must be Missing an Angel [Article 42]
18. Mark Morrison - Return of the Mack [Article 44]

# Gas on Tour – 2015/16 Away Game Statistics

| Club | Official Total of Gasheads | Total Crowd | Miles (one way, from Bristol) | Other QI Factors AT = All Ticket SO = Sold Out |
|---|---|---|---|---|
| Yeovil Town | 2,038 | 5,895 | 41 | AT for Gas |
| Luton Town | 553 | 8,061 | 133 | AT for Gas. Tuesday night. |
| Leyton Orient | 1,023 | 5,777 | 158 | |
| Plymouth Argyle | 1,587 | 10,633 | 131 | AT for Gas – SO |
| Hartlepool United | 190 | 3,788 | 287 | Tues night for longest away trip of the season! |
| Morecambe | 386 | 1,712 | 230 | |
| Mansfield Town | 847 | 4,197 | 166 | AT for Gas |
| Cambridge United | 562 | 5,115 | 183 | Changed at relatively short notice to Friday evening. Also shown live at the Mem, where circa 700 watched on. |
| Southend United (JPT) | 181 | 3,495 | 174 | £10 for adults. Changed at relatively short notice from Tuesday night to Wed night |
| Crawley Town | 836 | 2,612 | 145 | |
| Exeter City | 1,559 | 5,548 | 102 | AT for Gas – SO |
| Dagenham & Redbridge | 603 | 1,820 | 160 | |
| AFC Wimbledon | 806 | 4,668 | 125 | Boxing Day – No trains running. Wasn't AT for either set of fans, BUT whole ground was full by late lunchtime on match day |
| Barnet | 1,262 | 2,764 | 125 | |
| Oxford United | 2,359 | 9,492 | 86 | Sunday. AT for everyone – Original allocation sold out. Extra 300 almost sold out. |
| Accrington Stanley | 543 | 2,027 | 199 | |
| Portsmouth | 2,863 | 17,808 | 95 | AT for Gas – SO |
| Wonky Wanderers | 1,629 | 4,759 | 103 | AT for Gas |
| Notts. County | 1,108 | 5,052 | 140 | |
| Newport County | 1,042 | 3,663 | 39 | AT for Gas – SO immediately |
| Carlisle United | 651 | 4,718 | 276 | Easter Monday. 2nd longest away trip of the season. Thanks Football League. |
| Northampton Town | 925 | 7,579 | 112 | AT for Gas – SO. Also shown live at a sold out Mem, where circa 1,700 watched. |
| Stevenage | 1,327 | 3,836 | 146 | Tuesday night |
| York City | 2,000 | 4,525 | 225 | AT for Gas – SO. Late decision made to also show it live at the Mem, which also sold out. |
| **TOTAL** | **26,937** | **127,724** | **3,581** | |

# thanks & acknowledgements

☠ Many thanks to James McNamara at the Bristol Post who continued to publish my articles on their web site, and was supportive and encouraging throughout. There is no way I would have continued for over two years, nor put so much effort into them, if they weren't being seen by the public each week.

☠ Special thanks to my brother Chris and my best friend Mike, who often gave positive feedback and encouragement as I crawled along week after week, trying to think of new angles and vaguely entertaining topics.

☠ Thanks to all the Gasheads who offered me the use of their photographs to brighten up the book. The ones used in this finished book were supplied by Chris Bull, Rich Clark, Steve Collett, Wayne Collins, Steve Ford, David Johnson, Mark & Oscar Lewis, Alan Long, & Rick Weston.

☠ A general thanks to all the Gas forums, and their administrators / moderators (a truly thankless task if there ever was one!), who played a part in this book just by their very existence. It would have been hard for me to get in touch with so many interested Gasheads and photo contributors without such outlets for publicity and messages.

# about the author

Martin Bull became a Gashead in 1989 whilst falling in love with Twerton Park and standing near G pillar. Having been exiled for much of his past away games have always been special for him, so much so that in 2014 during a general slump in positivity about Rovers, he deliberately went the other way and collected and edited the away day experiences of over 40 fellow Pirates for the acclaimed book, 'Away The Gas'.

In late April 2014 he arranged to start writing a weekly online article for the Bristol Post newspaper, entitled 'G is for Gas', assuming he would soon be chronicling yet another dreary struggle in League Two. As karma dished up a humiliating relegation it also invited a tilt at redemption, and the 55 un-edited articles from that unique season formed the basis of his fifth book, 'Print That Season!', the antidote to obedient season reviews, with none of the hindsight that most football writers rely on.

Back in 2006 Martin was the first to offer (free) tours around London's most arty streets and wrote, photographed and published 'Banksy Locations & Tours' the first independent book about the artist Banksy.

He's been involved in publications on and off for over 20 years but that book was his first fully published work. It became a DIY favourite and is on its 5th Edition in the UK and 2nd edition in the rest of the world. A Korean version also apparently exists but he has never seen it; rather like a goal by Steve Yates.

A majestic Volume 2 was released in 2010 and other books have recently followed, including shamelessly jumping on the adult colouring band wagon with an innovative 'Banksy Colouring & Drawing Book'. Please buy it because he's skint.

Martin has donated £34,723 so far to charities through sales of his Banksy books and related fundraising initiatives, and hopes to be able to add more in the future.

Please feel free to contact him via twitter (@awaythegas) or email - hello@awaythegas.org.uk